D1492075

THE HOME UNIVERSITY LIBRARY
OF MODERN KNOWLEDGE

102

A HISTORY OF PHILOSOPHY

A History of
Philosophy

CLEMENT C. J. WEBB

Geoffrey Cumberlege
OXFORD UNIVERSITY PRESS
LONDON   NEW YORK   TORONTO

First published in 1915, *and reprinted in* 1919, 1920, 1922, 1924
(*twice*), 1925, 1927, 1929, 1931, 1933, 1937 *and* 1944
Reset in 1947 *and reprinted in* 1949 *and* 1951

CONTENTS

CHAPTER I

PHILOSOPHY AND ITS HISTORY

'WISE I may not call them; for that is a great name which belongs to God alone; *lovers of wisdom* or *philosophers* is their modest and befitting title.' So speaks Socrates in Plato's *Phaedrus* of the genuine teachers of mankind, who, whether they be poets or lawgivers or dialecticians like Socrates himself, know what they are talking about, and can distinguish what is really good from what is only apparently so, preferring what can be shown to be true to what is merely plausible and attractive. The word Philosophy has in the course of its long history been used now in a wider, now in a narrower sense; but it has constantly stood for inquiry not so much after certain particular facts as after the fundamental character of this world in which we find ourselves, and of the kind of life which in such a world it behoves us to live.

Sometimes a distinction has been drawn between *natural* and *moral* philosophy, according as attention is directed to the world, or to our life in it. In English books of a hundred years ago 'philosopher' more often than not meant a 'natural philosopher', and 'philosophy' what we should nowadays call 'natural science'. This may be explained by the fact that it was at that time a prevalent view in this country that, apart from what could be learned from a supernatural revelation, the inductive and mathematical methods used in the natural sciences were the only means we had for discovering the nature of the world; while (apart again from duties prescribed by supernatural authority) it was man's chief task to be, in Bacon's words, the 'minister and interpreter' of that 'Nature' whose ways by those methods he endeavoured to search out. On the other hand, in popular language a 'philosopher' often means no more than a person who in the conduct of his life is not at the mercy of circumstance. It is, no doubt, suggested that this is so because he has come to know the sort of world he has to do with, and so is not to be taken by surprise, whatever happens to him; yet the stress is laid rather on his behaviour than on the knowledge which has made it possible. Nowadays, we do not so commonly speak of 'natural philosophy' as of 'natural science'; and an astronomer or a physicist, a chemist or a biologist, we should not call a philosopher, unless, over and above his special researches, he were also to engage in some speculation as to the fundamental nature of the one world in which there is mind as well as matter, unity as well as multiplicity, individuality as well as general laws, and were to put to himself such questions as these: How are matter and mind mutually related? How can what is one be also many, and what is many be also one? What is an individual? How can what is not individual be real? and yet how can we describe any individual at all except in terms which might at any rate be applicable to other individuals as well? Such questions may be provoked by the investigations of the natural sciences, but cannot be decided by the methods used in those investigations. So long as a scientific investigator does not raise questions of this kind, he cannot, in our sense of the word, be called a philosopher; though he may perhaps be so called, if, having raised them, he arrives after consideration at the conclusion that they are unanswerable and therefore not worth raising again.

Philosophy, says Plato, begins with wonder; and, certainly, no kind of animal could learn to philosophize but one whose nature it was not to take things as they come, but to ask after the why and the wherefore of each, taking for granted that each *has* a why and a wherefore, and seeing in whatever happens to him (though he might not put it in this language) no isolated fact, but an instalment of a single experience, a feature of a single encompassing reality, within which all else that had happened or might happen would also be included. But we should hardly call this wonder or curiosity by the name of Philosophy until it had passed beyond the childish stage at which it could find satisfaction in mere stories, such as we find in the mythologies of all nations, which explain the origin of the world on the analogy of processes familiar to us as happening within the world, but which we cannot conceive as taking place outside of the world. As Professor Burnet has observed (*Early Greek Philosophy*, p. 10), the real advance made by the men whom we reckon as the founders of European philosophy 'was that they left off telling tales. They gave up the hopeless task of describing what was when as yet there was nothing, and asked instead what all things really are now'.

The men of whom he is here speaking are the members of a school of inquirers who in the sixth century before our era flourished at Miletus, a prosperous city founded by Ionian Greeks on the coast of Asia Minor. It is with these men that our history of philosophy must begin. It is doubtful whether a philosophy properly so called—that is, a systematic inquiry into the true nature of the world, set on foot merely for the sake of knowing the truth about it—can be shown to have originated anywhere independently of the ancient Greeks. Speaking of social life, R. R. Marett said (*Anthropology*,[1] p. 185): 'To break through custom by the sheer force of reflection, and so to make rational progress possible, was the intellectual feat of one people, the ancient Greeks; and it is at least highly doubtful if, without their leadership, a progressive civilization would have existed today.' To the same people we owe, in like manner, that disuse of mere customary repetition of traditional explanations of the world's origin and structure, in favour of free speculation and investigation, which has made possible science and philosophy, as we now understand those words. Hence we are justified in beginning our history of philosophy with the earliest group of Greek thinkers with whose theories we have any acquaintance. And even were there better evidence than there is of the existence of a genuine philosophy wholly independent of that which arose among the Greeks, it would still be impossible within the compass of the present book to attempt more than a description of that succession of thinkers who stand in a direct historical connexion with the development of modern European thought and knowledge; and the first in that succession are undoubtedly the ancient Greek philosophers.

With the Greek philosophers, therefore, our history will begin. From their time onward to our own, there

[1] Home University Library.

has been carried on within the sphere of European civilization a constant discussion of the kind of problems which we call philosophical, with a conscious reference to the conclusions reached by the chief Greek thinkers. This discussion has been at different times carried on more or less actively, more or less freely, more or less strictly within the lines laid down by its originators. There have been, as Bacon has said, waste and desert tracts of time, wherein the fruits of civilization, philosophy among them, have not been able to flourish. During these the discussion of philosophical problems has flagged; those who carried it on at all have but repeated the old arguments, and even of the old arguments themselves many have been forgotten or misunderstood.

Again, the discussion has not always been carried on with perfect freedom, without fear of the issue, 'whithersoever', to use a phrase of Plato's, 'the argument may lead us'. It has sometimes been supposed that a supernatural authority has on certain points enlightened us with information which we could not contradict without committing the sin of disloyalty to a divine teacher. Sometimes, again, the very increase of knowledge as to the views of earlier philosophers has hindered those that came after from thinking questions out for themselves. Sometimes, on the other hand, new experiences, religious, moral, political, economic, scientific, aesthetic, have given a new direction to men's thoughts, and turned their attention away from the teaching of their predecessors to the facts; whether to facts which those predecessors had also had before them, or to others which had not been within their ken. At such times there has often been loss as well as gain. Mistakes which had long ago been corrected have been revived; and old confusions have been given a new lease of life under new names.

Thus the History of Philosophy, which we shall attempt to summarize, although it is the history of a discussion constantly carried on from the sixth century before the Christian era to the twentieth century after it, is not the history of a discussion in which every point made is made once for all, or every step taken is a step forward. Rather, it is the history of a discussion subject to interruption by practical affairs, interspersed with digressions more or less irrelevant to its main topic, conducted now slackly and now keenly, by disputants of very various abilities. Yet, when we survey it as a whole, we shall find that it is a discussion in which a real progress can be detected; and in which even interruptions and digressions have proved refreshing and suggestive.

CHAPTER II

PLATO AND HIS PREDECESSORS

THE problem upon which the philosophers of Miletus fixed their attention was that of change. Things were always coming into being and passing away, and yet they did not come from nothing, or pass away into nothing. The spectacle of the world was not a spectacle of new beginnings and utter vanishings; it was, rather, a spectacle of perpetual transformation—but transformation of what? What was this *one thing* which took so many various shapes? That was the question which the earliest Greek philosophers set themselves to solve.

The oldest of them whose name has come down to us, Thales, said that it was water. The next, Anaximander, said that it was a boundless or infinite substance out of which are segregated, so to speak, the different substances with which we have to do; not only water, which Thales had supposed to be the primary matter, but fire, which is its opposite and ever wages against it a truceless war. The third, Anaximenes, identified this primitive substance with air, or rather with mist or vapour, which could either be rarefied and heated into fire or condensed and cooled into water. All these three philosophers were citizens of Miletus, and all flourished in the sixth century before our era. Early in the next century, in the year 494 B.C., the invading Persians destroyed Miletus, and the Milesian school came to an end in its original home. But, at the not far distant city of Ephesus, there was then living a philosopher who must be reckoned as the successor of the Milesians. This was Heraclitus, whom later tradition called the 'weeping philosopher', because, it was said, he always found in human life matter for tears, whereas Democritus (of whom we have yet to speak) found rather matter for laughter.

Heraclitus saw in fire the primary substance. Do we not see how flame is perpetually nourished by fuel, and how it perpetually passes into smoke? The swiftness of flame, moreover, is so great that we may without absurdity think that man's swift thought is of like nature with it; and the confusion introduced into our wits by overmuch liquor may seem to confirm the suspicion. 'The dry soul is the best', he said; and when we speak nowadays of the 'dry light of science', the phrase is an echo of this ancient theory. The mind in ourselves is, then, a part of the eternal fire; and to this eternal fire can thus be attributed the power of thinking which characterizes our minds. But the great importance of Heraclitus in the history of philosophy is not due to this new answer of his to the old question about the primary substance. It is due to the stress which he laid on the unceasing process of flux or change in which, as he held, all things were involved. As the hymn compares Time, so Heraclitus compared the course of nature to 'an ever-rolling stream'. You cannot step twice, he said, into the same river; for the water into which you first stepped will by now have flowed on, and other water will have taken its place. Now it is easy to see that this doctrine of a universal flux involves very serious consequences for any one who should, above all things, desire *knowledge.* For how is knowledge possible if there is nothing that abides as it is; if, as soon as any statement is made, nay, before it is out of the speaker's mouth, it has ceased to be true? It was said that consistent Heracliteans renounced speech, and took to pointing instead. They criticized, we are told, their master Heraclitus himself as not having gone far enough in his saying that a man could not step twice into the same river; for, said they, he could not do it once, since not for one instant did it remain the *same* river.

It was to a certain Cratylus, who flourished a hundred years after Heraclitus himself, that these rigorous deductions from the doctrine of the universal flux are attributed; and of this Cratylus Plato (*b.* 427, *d.* 347) was in his youth a disciple. What he learned from this teacher concerning the flux in which all such things as can be perceived by the senses are involved, and concerning the consequent impossibility of really knowing them, stirred him up, it would seem, to seek elsewhere for something which should not be thus ever in process of becoming something else, but should admit of being *known* to be, essentially and permanently, of a certain nature. We must here note that Plato took the flux of Heraclitus to involve only such things as the senses could apprehend. This was because Heraclitus and his contemporaries had recognized no reality which was not corporeal. They were not, indeed, materialists, in the sense in which that word implies the express denial that there is any reality which is not corporeal; for no definite suggestion that such a reality exists had yet been made. They had not drawn a distinction which to us is apt to seem fundamental; they did not deny to mind the property of filling space, which belongs to matter; nor did they deny to matter the property of thinking, which belongs to mind. To Heraclitus the soul could be dry, and fire could be wise.

In what direction did Plato, in his dissatisfaction, a hundred years after Heraclitus, with the Ephesian philosopher's doctrine of the universal flux, and the consequences, so unacceptable to an ardent aspirant after knowledge, which Cratylus deduced from it, look for an abiding object whereof there could be a true knowledge? He looked, we are told, in a direction which had been indicated to him by Socrates.

Socrates the Athenian (b. about 470, d. 399) was one of several among the greatest teachers of our race who have left no writings of their own behind them, and whose teachings are known to us only through the reports of others, reports which it is not always easy to reconcile with one another even in points of great importance. In the case of Socrates, the chief of these reports are a caricature by the comic poet Aristophanes in his play *The Clouds*, which was first represented when Socrates was about fifty years old; a book of reminiscences (usually called the *Memorabilia*) written after the death of Socrates by the distinguished soldier Xenophon, the leader and historian of the famous retreat of the ten thousand Greek mercenaries in 401 B.C. from the Persian highlands to the sea; and the *Dialogues* of Plato. Plato, like Aristophanes and Xenophon and Socrates himself, was a native of Athens. As quite a young man he had become a disciple of Socrates, and when, in later life, he composed the wonderful presentations of philosophical arguments in dramatic form which have made

consented to let his friends contrive his escape from prison, it is likely that it could have been effected without difficulty, and he could have spent the remnant of his days in a comfortable exile. But he would not admit that he had deserved any penalty; though under protest he so far yielded to his friends' entreaty as to name a fine (of no great amount), he plainly said that the treatment which was really due to him was an honourable provision at the public expense as a benefactor to his country; and when, after this refusal to declare himself against his conscience to be anything but innocent, the death sentence was pronounced, he would not by evading it turn his back in his old age on the duty, which he had ever thought and practised, of filial submission to his country's laws. Of the closing scenes of his life Plato has given us in his *Apology*, *Crito*, and *Phaedo* a picture which, as a pattern of piety and courage in the presence of death, is one of the spiritual treasures of our race.

It would seem that neither of the two charges brought against him was true in its most obvious sense; but there was plausibility in both. What were the grounds alleged for the accusation of irreligion, we have no distinct information. But although, according to our evidence, religious nonconformity was no characteristic of Socrates, yet—even apart from probable failure in the popular mind (as in the Aristophanic caricature) to distinguish between various forms of the movement of free thought, of which Socrates was the most conspicuous figure, and the consequent attribution to him of a destructive rationalism with which he had little sympathy—his talk of a divine mission and of supernatural warnings peculiar to himself might well suggest that he was not content with the religion of his neighbours. Possibly also there were rumours of friendly relations existing between him and circles known to profess initiation in religious mysteries or secret rites unconnected with the State system of worship. As to the corruption of the youth, we may well believe, on the word of those who knew the facts, that the remarkable influence exercised over boys and young men by Socrates was one which made for right-eousness and self-control, and yet admit that suspicion might naturally be aroused by the intimate association with him in their youth of men (such as Alcibiades and Critias) who had afterwards become notorious for the unscrupulousness and disloyalty of their political careers. Nor, indeed, can the dissatisfaction with the failings of his own state, which, loyal citizen as he was alike in his life and in his death, Socrates certainly felt and expressed, have counted for nothing in un-settling his disciples' allegiance to the standards recognized by their fellow countrymen. It is note-worthy that, of his two chief apologists, Plato in many respects preferred to the constitution of Athens that of her rival Sparta, and Xenophon actually passed from the Athenian into the Spartan service.

There are few among the celebrated men of history with whose personal appearance and habits we are so well acquainted as with those of Socrates. Some reference to these is not out of place even in so brief a history of philosophy as this; for in his person Plato, the greatest of writing philosophers, saw incarnate the ideal of the philosophic life. The contrast between his ugly exterior and the nobility of his spirit pro-foundly impressed a people like the Athenians, who were peculiarly susceptible—and none more so than Socrates himself—to the charm which is added to intercourse with a beautiful soul when it is housed in a beautiful body. In a famous passage of Plato's *Banquet*, Alcibiades compares his master to an image of the grotesque and pot-bellied satyr Silenus, which, when opened, is found to contain the beautiful figure of some god. The same dialogue gives us a vivid account of Socrates' extraordinary powers of endurance and self-control, which enabled him to endure without defeat alike the utmost rigours of military service and the sharpest temptations of the flesh; to remain at the end of a drinking bout, in which he had by no means abstained from his share of the wine to which his companions had succumbed, as sober and clear-headed as ever; and during a campaign to meditate in complete abstraction from all surroundings through a whole winter's day and night. This singular capacity of rising above the weaknesses of other men was united in Socrates with a social charm, a keen humour, a critical perspicacity, which made it impossible to disregard him as an inhuman ascetic or an unpractical dreamer. His imposing personality, unaided as it was by rank or wealth or beauty, presented philosophy to the world in her native dignity; and the would-be philosopher, whether attracted more by the 'rigour of the game' of thinking things out, or by the desire to be independent of the changes and chances of this mortal life, could find either ideal exemplified in the great Athenian.

We have now to consider how it was that Socrates (as has been said) showed Plato the way out of the doubt of the very possibility of true knowledge into which he had been plunged by his assent to the doctrine of Heraclitus that all things were in a perpetual flux. We have seen that Socrates was contemporary with, and was regarded at Athens as representative of, a widespread rationalistic movement. The leaders of this movement were a class of men of whom we generally speak collectively as 'the Sophists'. The word 'sophist', which we now use to signify a dishonest reasoner, meant properly no more than a professor of wisdom or knowledge. To his contemporaries, Socrates was himself a 'sophist'; and it is as the arch-sophist that he is caricatured by Aristophanes. But the title was one which Socrates did not care to claim. To the possession of wisdom he made no pretensions, only to the love of it; when an enthusiastic disciple told him on the authority of the Delphic oracle that he was the wisest of men, he was seriously perplexed; and the constant cross-examination, to which he proceeded to devote himself, of all pretenders to wisdom that he could find, he represented as undertaken from a sense of religious duty, in order to satisfy himself as to the meaning of the god. The result of this cross-examination was a conviction that these pretenders knew no more than himself; and he concluded that he was, as the oracle had said, wiser than other men, not because he knew more, but because he was aware, as they were not, of his own ignorance. Further, it seemed to him that, even if one had possessed wisdom, it would have been wrong to make of it a means of worldly profit. The profession of it in this way by his contemporaries had led them to prefer popularity to thoroughness. Living by the applause of the public, they must needs say what the public liked. The public itself was the great Sophist, in the bad sense which his disciple Plato probably learned from him to give to the word, and which it still bears, of one who loves gainful plausibility rather than the genuine truth, which makes men free indeed, but not rich. He himself charged no fees for his instructions, and remained a poor man to the end.

Hence, while the world at large took Socrates for a notable sophist, his followers came to regard him as the great antagonist of those who could properly be so called. These were men who, for the most part, had detached themselves from civil ties and wandered from place to place (unlike Socrates who, except on military service, never left Athens), gathering pupils who hoped to learn from them the arts of persuasion by which they might achieve success in their respective commonwealths. Men associated with their instructions the spread of a notion that the distinction between right and wrong was not natural and permanent, but merely conventional, so that (as seemed, indeed, to be the case in view of the great variety of customs obtaining in different places) what was right in one country was wrong in another, and nothing was wrong but might become right if circumstances were changed. It appeared impossible any longer to identify (as simple old-fashioned folk were apt to do) right conduct with a particular set of customary or traditional rules of behaviour, without being brought up at once against exceptional cases, in which the rules would not hold. This disquieting criticism of familiar ways of thinking could not be permanently checked by refusing to consider these exceptional cases. It was the distinctive feature of Socrates' teaching that he sought by further thinking and discussion to heal the hurt that thinking and discussion had done to simple faith in moral principles. *This* is right, or just, or brave here and now—*that* there and then—*the other* under those other circumstances. Well and good; but, if these statements are to have any meaning at all, *right*, *just*, *brave* must mean the same in each case. We may, for example, admire some man's honesty on some particular occasion; yet we should readily admit that we might be mistaken as to his motives, and that a fuller acquaintance with them might make it plain that there was nothing to admire. I *thought* (we should say) that he was honest; but I fear I was mistaken. But we should resent the suggestion that we did not *know* what honesty was; and, if we did not, how could we recognize it or even mistakenly think that we recognized it, in the particular case before us? Hence our great business is to make clear to ourselves what we mean by these *predicates* (as they are called in logic, a science which owes much to these discussions)—*right*, *just*, *brave* and the rest—and to fix our meaning by a *definition* of each.

It was this assertion by Socrates that there were permanent natures of justice, courage, and so forth, which it was the purpose of framing definitions to express, that showed Plato a way of deliverance from the doubts about the possibility of knowledge induced in him by the Heraclitean doctrine. For these natures were not objects of the bodily senses. What I perceive with the bodily senses on each occasion is only a particular man or action in which I *think* I recognize a nature which I *know*; but this nature itself is an object, not of the senses, but of the understanding. There is, then (so Plato concluded), beside the world of sensible things, for ever shifting and changing—and even at once great and small, hot and cold (for such terms are always relative), so that what is said of them at any time is never lastingly, never wholly true—another world of eternal forms or natures, about which we can have *knowledge* properly so called, a knowledge which is presupposed in the very *opinions* which are all we can have about the things which are apprehended by the bodily senses. For I cannot even mistake another man for you, unless I know you; nor can I guess, even wrongly, that such and such an act or man is honest, unless I know what honesty is. Socrates (we are told) had confined his suggestions on this subject to the sphere of morality, that is to such definable natures as have been already instanced, to which it concerns all men to conform their actions, and with which it is thus of practical importance that they should be familiar. Plato, at any rate, carried the line of thought further, as he might easily do. For as, in order to *think* that this or that act is just, we must *know* what justice is; so, also, in order to *think* that the line A B is straight or that the lines A B and C D are equal, we must *know* what straightness or what equality is. Here, too, there is a permanent nature, apprehended by the understanding, not by the senses, which does not become, even while we speak of it, something else than what we are saying that it is. These permanent natures, discovered by Socrates in his efforts to find an abiding object for our moral judgements, which should not be at the mercy of custom and circumstance, became the corner-stone of Plato's philosophy, and are called by him Forms or, to use the Greek word, Ideas.

This word Idea is familiar to us; but in modern English it usually means something very different from what it meant to Plato. With us, it means something in our minds which may or may not correspond to an independent reality outside of them. With him, it meant the form—not the mere outward shape, but the inner essential structure or nature of anything, which made it the kind of thing it was. Even when it was what we call a corporeal or material thing, it was not the senses (which have only to do with superficial appearances) that could take account of this inner essential nature. The Form or Idea is, therefore, the proper object, not of the senses, but of the understanding. Yet we must be careful to remember that this does not mean that it is what we call a 'notion' or 'concept', something which has its being only in the mind; it is that of which we have a notion or concept, but which does not by any means depend for its existence upon our thinking of it. We may help ourselves to remember this by recalling the way in which the modern man of science commonly regards the 'laws of nature' which it is his task to discover. He does not think of them, of course, as bodily substances which he perceives or might perceive with his senses; but neither does he think that their existence depends upon his or any one being aware of them. His 'science' consists in ascertaining and describing what they are. If his senses report anything inconsistent with an ascertained law, he is more inclined to suspect that they are deceived than that the law is not what his understanding (starting, no doubt, from experiences got by means of the senses) has made it out to be. It would not, indeed, be correct to say that what Plato meant by Ideas is just what the modern man of science means by 'laws of nature'; but the consideration of our attitude towards the latter may help us to understand Plato's view of the former. The Ideas of Plato are the eternal natures, whatever they be, which constitute the inner reality of the universe, and which alone can be objects of true knowledge. They are not perceptible by the senses; they can be apprehended by the understanding only. But, just as we commonly take the things which the senses perceive to have an existence quite independent of our perception of them, so the Platonic Ideas are no product of the mental activity by means whereof we apprehend them; they are rather its presupposition.

It was said of Bacon that he 'would light his torch at every man's candle'. The saying is eminently true also of Plato, whose genius found stimulus and suggestion in the teaching of many predecessors beside Heraclitus and Socrates. Thus, he owed much to the Pythagoreans, with some of whom his master Socrates seems to have lived on terms of friendship. This school of thinkers took their name from Pythagoras, who was born in the middle of the sixth century at Samos, an island off that coast of Asia Minor where the earliest Greek philosophers taught, but who spent the latter part of his life among the Greek colonies to which Southern Italy owed its title of Magna Graecia, or Greater Greece.

Pythagoras left, it would seem, no writings behind him, but was the founder of a religious society, which in one city of that region, Crotona, succeeded in acquiring for a time the supreme control of the common-wealth. The Milesian school of thinkers had been at no pains to connect their philosophy with the popular religion; though they spoke of 'gods', they meant by the words not conscious beings to be worshipped, but merely the principal elements of the system of material nature. But Pythagoras was the leader of a religious revival which, if, on the one hand, it brought into new prominence certain superstitious beliefs and practices of primitive, not to say savage, origin, on the other hand deepened the sense of individual dignity and responsibility by its doctrine of the immortality and transmigration of souls. He was at the same time, like the Milesians themselves, a man of science, and is reckoned as the founder of the science of geometry and as the discoverer of the musical octave. Among those who in Plato's day called themselves Pythagoreans, there lived on both the tradition of mathematical and musical studies, and the tradition of a serious interest in the destiny of individual souls. The latter tradition was connected with the speculations and fancies contained in certain books which passed under the name of the mythical musician Orpheus, to whom legend attributed a special knowledge of the secrets of the world beyond the grave.

On both its mathematical and its religious sides, Pythagoreanism exercised a considerable influence upon Plato. He was himself a great mathematician, and is said to have put this inscription over the door of his lecture-room: 'No admission to any one ignorant of Geometry.' His account of the Ideas, eternal natures which do not come into being or pass away, nor are in any way affected by the lapse of time, had been in many respects anticipated by the Pythagorean doctrine that the ultimate essence of reality was to be sought in Numbers. To this doctrine Pythagoras' discovery that musical harmonies depend upon numerical proportions perhaps first gave occasion; and the progress of natural science, which was perpetually extending the range of exact measurement, and describing in mathematical formulas an ever-increasing number of natural phenomena, would continually confirm it. Among the eternal natures which Plato called Ideas must certainly be included many natures beside those of the numbers and figures with which the mathematician deals; yet we know that Plato himself, and still more the first generation of his followers, were wont, in the spirit of the Pythagoreans, to speak of them all, whenever they could, in mathematical language.

A like relationship to that which connects Plato's doctrine of Ideas with the Pythagorean doctrine of Numbers connects his doctrine of the Soul with the Pythagorean speculations on its immortality and transmigrations. For Plato, the Soul is the link between the eternal and unchanging world of the Ideas, which by its understanding or reason it is able to apprehend and survey, and the world in which birth and death, death and birth, succeed one another in a perpetual cycle. Of the movement and change which characterize this inferior world, the living Soul is, according to Plato, the cause; for it is the only thing, he holds, that we can think of as spontaneously moving itself and originating movement in other things: bodies can only move when pushed by others, or when, as in living beings, set going by a soul or principle of life within them. Plato could not think but that the Soul must share the eternity of those Ideas in the apprehension whereof lay its essential nature and function as a mind or intelligence; while, although the individual beings, which in the course of the cycle of birth and death are incessantly coming into existence or passing away, can lay no claim to permanence, the cycle itself and the Soul which is the principle of its perpetual movement are without beginning or end. But this immortal or eternal Soul is the *Anima mundi*, or Soul of the world; it is not your individual soul or mine; for these belong to the cycle of birth and death, and include, along with the apprehension of the eternal Ideas, all sorts of imaginations and desires which have their origin in the perishable bodies with which our souls are associated.

What, then, did Plato hold concerning the origin and destiny of your soul or mine? In trying to answer this question, it is necessary to remind ourselves that, in Plato's view, Philosophy is the apprehension of eternal and unchanging natures, and the only questions which she can properly be called upon to answer are questions about these, and not about the past history or future prospects of anything which is affected by the lapse of time. There must be, of course, a true answer to questions of this latter kind; but all that Philosophy can say of them is that neither of the past nor of the future can anything be true which is not in accordance with what she knows of the eternal and unchanging natures. Hence, in cases where there is at hand no historian or prophet who can tell us what has been or is to be, we must be content to fashion for ourselves a 'myth' or story, of which it is required only that it should nowhere contradict what we know to be the eternal nature of things. The *Dialogues* of Plato contain a number of such 'myths', which suggest answers to questions of just this sort—questions about the creation of the world, or the origin of society, or the destiny of the individual soul. For these last, Plato drew upon the traditions connected with the name of Orpheus, and the kindred speculations of Pythagoras and his followers. There is no reason to doubt that, while giving rein to his imagination in the details, he really believed as a matter of probable opinion, though not (since it concerned the world of vicissitude) as a part of the knowledge attainable by philosophical discussion properly so called, that even individual souls never wholly perished.

The apparent *recognition* of truth when presented to the individual for the first time—as when we say of the solution of a mathematical problem, 'Yes, I see that is right'—seemed to him best explained by the supposition that one is really recalling what had been known to us in a previous state of existence, but since forgotten. Perhaps every soul passed through a series of re-incarnations, in which the nature of each new birth was determined by the moral character acquired in the one preceding. A somewhat similar belief forms an important article of the Buddhist creed; which, however, sets before its followers the hope of an ultimate deliverance, through the accumulation of merit in successive lives, from the necessity of being born again at all. Plato, since he does not regard life in Buddhist fashion as necessarily an evil, does not speculate upon such an escape from the cycle of birth and death. But he is earnestly concerned to insist that the eternal nature of things requires the destiny of any soul to be decided according to its deserts. The doctrine that the gods can be bribed by money spent on sacrifices to let the sinner off the consequences of his sin excites his strongest indignation; and, when he uses the language of the Orphic poems about an initiation which has the promise of a better life to come, he makes it plain that he has in mind no admission to assist as performer or spectator at external ceremonies, but the entry upon the life of a true philosopher, in which the eternal nature of goodness is understood and the conduct of life conformed thereto.

Beside the Pythagoreans, another school of philosophers, which had arisen later on in the same part of the Greek world, must be reckoned among those to which Plato was specially indebted. This was the Eleatic school, so called from the south Italian town of Elea or Velia, of which its first teacher, Parmenides, was a citizen. Plato introduces him, in a dialogue which bears his name, as visiting Athens when Socrates was a very young man, that is, in the middle of the fifth century B.C. In dealing with the same problem as Heraclitus, Parmenides took exactly the opposite line. Movement and change, which Heraclitus saw everywhere, he will have to be nowhere. Wherever we seem to find them, we are victims of an illusion. If we think of what we mean by moving, whatever moves must move into some unoccupied space. It is true that it may do this by pushing out some other occupant; but if there were no unoccupied space anywhere, no movement could begin at all. Parmenides seems to have considered that to speak of a space where there was nothing at all would imply that 'nothing' was

'something'. This appeared to him to be unthinkable; and he was sure that nothing unthinkable could
be real; and, indeed, we do commonly assume that in
making a thing intelligible to ourselves we are finding
out what it really is. Hence, he did not shrink from
saying that movement and change of every kind were
illusory, and that what really existed must be one
unchanging, unmoving thing, the same everywhere and
in every direction, without any distinction of parts in
its unbroken unity. Our senses present us, it must be
admitted, with a very different sort of world; but the
senses, which, as all men admit, often deceive us, are
not to be trusted; we must correct them by our
reason, which can make nothing of a world of change.

We can understand how Plato, who himself had
found no satisfaction for the aspirations of his reason
in the theory of a world wherein was nothing but
change, would be disposed to sympathize with
Parmenides. Indeed, in his own doctrine each single
Idea or eternal nature stands to the many sensible
things or facts, in which it is as it were repeated over
and over again, although mixed up with other and even
opposite characteristics, very much as the one Reality
of Parmenides stands to the illusory world of manifold
changing and moving things which the senses put
before us. But in Plato there is not only one eternal
nature, but many; there is, therefore, a multiplicity
and difference in the real and intelligible world as well
as the world of confused appearance which the senses
perceive; and, moreover, in Plato this world of appearance is not a mere illusion; it is 'between being and not
being'; it is really there before us, though it seems to
be what it is not; it is not, as Parmenides had made it

out to be, sheer 'not-being', without reality of any kind.

Parmenides' denial of the reality of so obvious a fact as movement no doubt seemed to his contemporaries highly paradoxical. A pupil of his, Zeno by name, sought to defend his master's paradox by showing that, when we try to understand this obvious fact of movement, we find it at least as paradoxical as Parmenides' doctrine that there is really no such thing. For example, if the swift-footed Achilles should run a race with a tortoise, it would at first seem easy to show that he must soon outstrip it. But let us see. Suppose Achilles to run ten times as fast as the tortoise, and the tortoise to have a hundred yards start. When Achilles has covered the hundred yards, the tortoise will be ten ahead; when Achilles has covered the ten, it will be one yard ahead; when Achilles has covered the one yard, the tenth of a yard; and so on, to infinity. Another of Zeno's puzzles is that of the moving arrow. At any instant of the time during which it is in motion, it will be at rest in a particular place; a cinematograph film might represent its flight by a series of instantaneous photographs in each of which it would so appear. When, then, does it move from one of these successive positions to the next? These and similar puzzles have proved of much importance as helping to show that extension in space and duration in time must both be regarded as continuous, and not as discrete, quantities; that is, they are not made up of points and instants as a number is made up of units.

Such a discussion of familiar notions, intended to bring out their difficulties by seeing what will follow if one admits the position of any one with whom one is arguing, is what the Greeks called *dialectic*, and of dialectic Zeno was considered the inventor. Socrates was a master of this art, and Plato was so convinced that it was the proper method, not of finding out particular facts, but of getting to the bottom of whatever view it brought forward, that he sometimes used the word *dialectic* for the science of the ultimate nature of reality, which we call Philosophy. In his *Dialogues*, the various positions from which he starts are put dramatically into the mouths of men who might naturally hold them. His earlier dialogues are suggested by the arguments of Socrates about the meaning of justice, courage, piety, and the like; in the later, where he is often concerned with more abstract conceptions, such as unity, identity, difference, and so forth, he is conscious that he is engaged on problems more like those which occupied the Eleatics. Accordingly Socrates is no longer unquestionably the central figure of the piece; Parmenides himself or an 'Eleatic stranger' takes a part in the discussion no less important than his.

One more predecessor of Plato must here be mentioned—Anaxagoras, who lived in the earlier half of the fifth century B.C. He was, like the Milesian philosophers before him, an Ionian Greek of Asia Minor, but lived for some years at Athens as the friend and adviser of the great statesman Pericles. He was at last, however, forced to leave that city, for the boldness of his speculations concerning the sun and moon, which he regarded not as divine beings but as bodies made of the same kind of stuff as the earth under our feet, had incurred the suspicion of the Athenian democracy. That democracy then, as in the case of Socrates a generation later, showed itself impatient of freedom of thought on subjects touching the religion of the State. Especially this was so when, as with both Anaxagoras and Socrates, this free thinking was practised in circles the distinction of whose members rendered uneasy a sensitive public, ready to scent political danger in any kind of social or personal superiority whatever.

The early attempts to explain the world about us by pointing to some single primitive substance, of which one could assert that everything at bottom was just *this*, had failed to account for the variety which the actual world exhibits. 'It takes', as the English proverb says in another connexion, 'all sorts to make a world.' How are we, then, the better off for an explanation which mentions only one sort? Anaxagoras allowed that things were originally of different sorts; but these different sorts were, he thought, all at first mixed up together in a confused mass or chaos, from which they were afterwards sorted out, and a proper place assigned to each. To what was this sorting out to be ascribed? Anaxagoras replied: 'To Mind or Intelligence.' This answer, we are told, made, when he first met with it, a great impression upon Socrates. It seemed to him a new and a more hopeful way than those suggested by other thinkers of explaining the wonderful order which we find in the world. To use an illustration of later date, if we were to find on the sea-shore a thing of complicated structure, the like of which we had never seen before, our curiosity would be satisfied if we learned that its structure enabled it to show the time of day, and that it was made by an intelligent human being who had designed it for that very purpose. Socrates, indeed, complained that Anaxagoras, having spoken of Intelligence as the general cause of the order of the world, did not go on to explain the details of its arrangement by the purposes they served. He tried to do this for himself, and was thus among the earliest of those who have set themselves to trace as best they could, in the adaptation of the bodies of men and animals to their mode of life, evidence that they are the handiwork of a wise and beneficent creator.

Plato was in close sympathy with his master here. When we are puzzled by anything which we observe, we try to find some way of regarding it which will puzzle us no longer, and at the same time show us why it puzzled us before. We trust our intelligence more than our senses, and are ready to say that the thing before us is *really* what we can understand, though it may still *look* very different. It is thus that we rise from the world which the senses perceive to the world of Ideas or eternal natures, wherein is no inconsistency or contradiction, but all is intelligible. There are, as we have seen, many such Ideas or eternal natures. Have they nothing to do with one another? The mind in quest of the intelligible will not be content to think so. It can only rest when it has found them all to be members of a single system, in which each has a place assigned to it by a principle which determines the function, the *good* of each. The vision of such a principle, an 'Idea of the Good', is the ultimate goal of our intellectual endeavour. Such a principle can be no mere creation of our fancy, unless the long quest to which is due the attainment of all our knowledge, whether that by which we distinguish the common objects of everyday life from mere reflections, shadows, imitations of them, or the exacter knowledge which we call science, has from the first been all astray. For we have always assumed that only what satisfies our intelligence can be real. And our intelligence cannot be satisfied unless it be assured that, in the last resort, it is no accident that things are intelligible, but that, if we have discovered what they are by following this clue, our justification is that Intelligence, akin to the intelligence which has hitherto guided our search, is the ground at once of their being what they are, and of their being known to us as they are; in other words, that there is immanent in them a divine plan, which is revealing itself to us, as, in the adventurous spirit of Socrates, we 'follow the argument whithersoever it lead us'.

Since only through acquaintance with this universal plan can a sure foundation be obtained for that knowledge of the due place of each of the several functions the performance of which makes up the life of an organized community of men—and except in an organized community human beings cannot develop their spiritual capacities—the rulers of such communities should, in Plato's judgement, be philosophers. In his greatest work, the *Republic*, he has sketched the training which would provide the State with 'guardians' so qualified. It is no merely intellectual training which he describes. It was characteristic of him not to think of the life of thought as something apart from the life of feeling or of will. The genuine philosopher will bring to the contemplation of the Supreme Goodness not only a mind trained in the exact sciences, but a passionate enthusiasm learned in the school of the love which beauty kindles in the young, and an unselfish public spirit ingrained by military discipline and by the habit of a comradeship in which a man (or a woman, for Plato's 'guardians' may be of either sex) may call nothing his or her own—not even (strange and monstrous as it seems to us) wife or husband, parent or child.

When Plato died in 347 B.C., he left behind him at Athens a college of his own foundation, called by the name already belonging to the place in which it was established, the Academy. This institution, whose name has come to be a synonym for 'learned society', became from the first a centre of scientific and philosophical activity. It was the nucleus of what in a later age developed into what we should call a university, and its corporate existence lasted until the confiscation of its endowments by the Emperor Justinian in A.D. 529. Among the young men who studied at this college under the founder himself, the most celebrated was he who became that founder's chief critic and the great rival of his fame, Aristotle of Stagira in Thrace.

CHAPTER III

ARISTOTLE AND OTHER SUCCESSORS
OF PLATO

IT has been said that every one is born either a Platonist
or an Aristotelian; and the names of the two great
Greek philosophers are often opposed to one another
as representative of two contrasted and incompatible
types of mind. Plato, it is thought, stands for the
'mystical' or 'idealistic' type, which supposes the
facts of life to mean more than meets the eye or ear,
and overleaps the bounds which nature has set to
experience, in order to speculate on things which are
guessed to lie beyond. Aristotle, on the other hand,
is taken for the champion of a more cautious method,
which, holding fast by the rules of a strict logic and
keeping close to the facts of experience, reaches positive
results, verifiable by observation and experiment, and
which shuns the regions of vague speculation in which
the Platonist, it is said, loves to expatiate. As in
Raphael's cartoon of the School of Athens, Plato
points upward to heaven, Aristotle downward to the
earth. A closer acquaintance with the great writers
in question might probably shake the reader's confidence in the accuracy of this popular view. He would
find Plato at once a severer reasoner and a more
practical moralist than it would suggest; while he
might be led to doubt whether Aristotle's temperance
in speculation and condescension to the ideals of
ordinary men had not been exaggerated.

Aristotle (*b.* 384, *d.* 322) was a member of Plato's

college, but became dissatisfied with the style of thought and teaching which prevailed there, and left it to found a similar institution of his own, in a place called the Lyceum; whence what in England is called a 'public school' is called to-day in France a *Lycée*. But, though he thus separated himself from those who had been his fellow scholars, Aristotle always, in his philosophical writings, starts from the position of a Platonist, and proceeds to develop his own views in the form of a criticism of those Platonic doctrines with which he found himself unable to agree. Hence, the first impression made upon a student is that of a perpetual opposition to Plato; the fundamental agreement in many respects between the pupil and his master is less observed, because it is, naturally, less insisted upon.

Aristotle agreed with Plato that the objects of knowledge, properly so called, were the permanent natures of things, which are apprehended not by the senses but by the understanding. These he called 'Forms', as Plato had done; but, while Plato had employed almost indifferently two very similar Greek words with this meaning, one of which was 'Idea', Aristotle rarely made use of this latter word, except when referring to the special views of Plato concerning them. Hence it is that the word 'Idea' has in the tradition of philosophy become especially associated with Plato. Aristotle took exception to the language, used by Plato and by most of his school, which represented the permanent natures of beings in the world around us as though they existed separately from the individual things which 'partook of' them or 'copied' them. Plato himself had, indeed, been aware of the inadequacy of these ways of stating the relation of the many things which there may be of any one kind to the nature which we recognize in them all, and which we can consider by itself apart from any particular instance of it. We may call this relation 'participation'; but we do not suppose the nature in question to be parcelled out among the instances of it so that, of many beings that we call, say, 'great' or 'small', each should have only a part of greatness or smallness dealt out to it, as, when several men take refuge under one sail, each is covered by a different bit of it. Or we may call the relation of this common nature to the instances of it 'imitation'. But, if I suppose the fact that you and I are both men to be explicable only by saying that we are both copies of one pattern, of an archetypal man, we shall have next to explain the likeness of each of us to that same pattern by saying that there is some further pattern, from which you or I and the archetypal man are copied, and so on to infinity. Perhaps the best answer to these difficulties would be that with the relation of a particular instance of a certain nature to that nature we are just as familiar as we are with the relation of a part to a whole or of a copy to its original. We do not understand any one of these the less because we cannot describe it in terms of another; or understand it the better because we try so to describe it. But if this was what Plato meant us to infer from the fact that he admitted the difficulties of such descriptions, while holding fast to his assertion that the natures of which there were many instances were yet real on their own account, he did not so plainly draw the conclusion as to make his followers renounce the questionable language about the particulars being copies of the common nature which he himself had sometimes used, or to satisfy Aristotle that this questionable language did not need to be decisively repudiated, if we were to reach a true comprehension of the relation of the common nature to the particular instances of it.

Aristotle did not suppose, as many have done, that the common nature could be dismissed as no more than a notion or conception of ours. This suggestion is actually put by Plato, in his dialogue *Parmenides*, into the mouth of the youthful Socrates. Parmenides at once disposes of it by the pertinent question: 'Is it a notion of nothing?' We should have, if we admitted it, to allow that the natural sciences, which deal almost wholly with characteristics common to many individuals, were a mere mind-play of ours, and could make no pretension to deal with realities independent of our minds. Aristotle, at any rate, did not deny that the Forms or permanent natures of things were independent of our minds. But he distinguished in the nature of things characteristics which were substantial (such as humanity) from characteristics which were only attributive (such as greatness, whiteness, wisdom, and the like). The latter were only real as belonging to the former; while of the substantial forms themselves he held that only in our discourse were they ever separated from the individual beings whose essential natures they were. Each individual being, indeed, might be said to have its own 'form'; in the case of a man this is what we otherwise call his 'soul'. His body, considered apart from the soul or principle of life to which it owes the structure and

functions which entitle it to be called a body, is the
opposite of the 'form'; it is the 'matter'. When
several things are of the same 'kind' or 'species'
(Aristotle here uses the same word which we have
hitherto translated by 'form'), no statement of permanent scientific value can be made of one such thing,
as a member of the species, which cannot as well be
made of another. The predicates in such statements,
which will hold of many individuals, he called
'universals', as opposed to 'particulars'; and hence
we often speak of Plato's Ideas, or Aristotle's Forms,
or whatever corresponds to these predicates, as
'universals'.

It is only, according to Aristotle, in the sublunary
world that there are many individuals belonging to
one and the same species. This is because bodies
below the moon are composed of a material compounded out of four kinds of substance, earth, water,
air and fire, the recognition of which as elements was
due to Empedocles, a very influential fifth-century
philosopher, whose home was Sicily, and who, according to a legend (which Matthew Arnold took for the
subject of a well-known poem), threw himself into the
crater of Etna, in order that so complete a disappear-
ance might encourage the belief that he had been
translated without dying to the company of the gods.
These four elements, themselves due to combinations
of what were regarded as the four fundamental
qualities, hot with its opposite cold, and moist with its
opposite dry, were tempered together in various proportions to form various bodies, which in view of the
constant opposition between their constituents could
have no lasting stability, and must therefore be perish-

able. Hence the multiplication of individuals, through the succession of which the species, though not the individual, could realize the immortality after which all things are consciously or unconsciously striving. In the higher regions of the universe, each individual heavenly body, being made not of this composite matter, but wholly of a superior stuff, the 'quintessence' or fifth element, is imperishable, and is the sole individual of its kind, not needing to secure immortality by begetting another individual of the same nature as itself.

This summary sketch will sufficiently show that it was chiefly to the phenomena of organic life that Aristotle's attention was directed; and it was to them, also, that he went for a clue whereby to explain what he held to be the eternal circular motion of the heavens. Where motion is due, as in inanimate bodies, to impact, the impingeing body must itself have been moved by the impact of another, and so on for ever. But in living beings we find another kind of motion. Plato, too, had sought for the ultimate source of movement in a living soul which moved itself. But Aristotle did not think the motion of living beings could be strictly described as self-movement. Their movement has always a cause beyond itself which acts on them not by pushing their bodies, but by exciting their desires, and need not itself be in motion at all. For desire may be of an object which does not reciprocate it, or is even unconscious of it. In the last resort, then, all motion must go back to an unmoved mover, who moves by exciting a desire which in turn brings about a movement of the living being in whom it is excited. And so, for Aristotle, ' 'Tis love, 'tis love that makes the world go round.' The unmoved mover of the universe is God. God, as supremely good, moves the world as the beloved moves the lover; but he does not reciprocate the love that draws all else toward him. The only activity which can be attributed to such a being, perfect and in need of nothing beyond himself, is that of knowledge; and the only object of knowledge which is not unworthy of him is his own eternally perfect nature. God is not the maker of the world, which is itself eternal; nor yet is he its soul; he is rather the perfect being which it yearns, so far as it can, to imitate.

In the case of things which are not eternal, and are subject (as the heavens, in Aristotle's view, are not) to that kind of change, from a more imperfect to a more perfect form, which we call development, he always seeks the ground of the earliest stages in the result towards which they tend. This is often called his 'teleology', or explanation of things by their end or 'final cause'. The final cause of organic beings is commonly sought by him not in their utility to man, but in their own perfection after their kind. Aristotle distinguished four kinds of cause: the material, the formal, the efficient, the final. Thus, fully to explain the origin of a house, we should have to mention the bricks and stones out of which it was built, the form they have been made to assume, the builder who arranged them thus, and the purpose of shelter which as so arranged they are enabled to serve. But on closer inspection all these, except the first, tend to coincide. For the builder is only a cause of the house so far as his mind conceived and his hands carried out the design of it; and it is only the particular kind of shelter that a house (and not, for example, a tent) affords which such a disposition of the material is fitted to provide. The efficient and final causes are thus—as could be shown even more clearly in the case of a work not of art, but of nature, such as an organism —alike aspects of the formal cause.

Thus this fourfold scheme does but elaborate the more fundamental distinction of two factors in all beings that are not eternal; a *matter*, which is capable of becoming what when invested with the form it actually becomes, and this *form*, in virtue of which we call the thing of that kind by the specific (not the individual) name belonging to it. (It is here to be remembered that *kind, species, form* are but different renderings of one and the same Greek word.) What has itself a form or characteristic nature of its own (e.g. marble) may become in its turn the matter or material of something else (e.g. a statue). We can never come face to face with mere matter; apart from some form or other, it would have no character, would be nothing at all. On the other hand, God is pure form without matter, since in his perfect life are no unrealized capacities, to be distinguished as matter from the spiritual activity of knowledge which is his essence. This activity of knowledge, which is the only one in Aristotle's view attributable without absurdity to God, he naturally regarded as the highest possible to man. Accordingly, in his *Ethics* the godlike life of knowledge is that in which man realizes his noblest capacity, whereby he is distinguished from all other denizens of the earth, and finds therein his greatest happiness. Only because man, in whom an animal nature is conjoined with the pure intellect, cannot lead this life without intermission, does human happiness involve also the exercise of the social and civic virtues. Man is, indeed, by nature a social animal; he is always found living in some sort of society, if only that of husband, wife, and children. But what Aristotle held to be the highest kind of life was only to be found in civilized communities of free citizens, such as, to his knowledge, men of Greek race alone had shown themselves capable of forming.

What is the best constitution for such a community he sets himself in his *Politics* to inquire. Although it was with a pupil of his own, Alexander the Great, that there begins for the Greek world a new period, in which the old city-states were reduced to subordinate membership in large empires, Aristotle does not seem to have anticipated the changed course which events were about to take. He still pictured a civilized state as a small independent commonwealth, occupying a single city with its adjacent territory, and not too large to allow of all its citizens taking a personal part in public affairs. Leisure for this purpose was to be secured to the citizens by the institution of domestic slavery, which Aristotle regarded as based upon the natural incapacity of some men for self-government. Whole nations exhibited this natural incapacity by setting up, when left to themselves, a despotic ruler, to whom all the rest stood in a servile relation. In the free commonwealth, political equality should correspond to real equality. To any member of the community who (like the 'heroes' of Carlyle) should be marked out by an intrinsic superiority to all the rest as their natural ruler, the others ought to submit.

Inequalities of wealth should not be ignored. With Plato's abolition of private property in the ruling class of his ideal state Aristotle was not in sympathy. The end which Plato had in view, the realization of the proverb that 'friends have all things in common', would not, Aristotle thought, be attained by such an arrangement. It is true that, in the intimacy of a close friendship, a man may know himself able without question to use what is his friend's as though it were his own; but this is quite a different matter from the common use by two men of something to one of whom it belongs no more than it does to the other; for such common use neither implies, nor does it always tend to produce, any particular friendship among those who enjoy it. Aristotle does not, then, exclude the possibility of one free citizen being richer than another. Wealth, he holds, gives to its possessors a 'stake in the country', which entitles them to a privileged position, sufficient to save them from lying at the mercy of those who have nothing, but not such as to enable them to reduce their poorer fellow-citizens to helpless dependence.

Various real inequalities having thus obtained due recognition, the general principle of government approved by Aristotle is that equal citizens should rule and be ruled, turn and turn about. If Aristotle does not, like Plato, desire to place the control of the State in the hands of philosophers, who are to order the concerns of the public in the light of their knowledge of the supreme principle of order in the universe, this is not because he takes a less exalted view of the functions of philosophy, but rather because he regards human conduct as belonging altogether to the world of change and decay, and hence as no concern of the higher philosophy, which deals with the eternal and immutable. Thus, he does not bring into so close a connexion as did Plato the lives of contemplation and of action, the man of science and the man of affairs. This is of a piece with his general tendency to find fault with Plato for laying stress on unity, on what things have in common, to the neglect of equally real and important differences. He regards himself as called to insist especially upon the latter. Each main department of knowledge, he holds, has principles of its own, which it shares with no other. There are, indeed, principles which obtain in all departments; of these the most universally applicable is the 'principle of contradiction', which says that nothing can be said at once to be and not to be the same thing at the same time in the same sense. But in no department can we gain positive knowledge by the help of these alone without taking into account the peculiar nature of its subject-matter. Thus Aristotle was led to render a great service to the progress of science by delimiting the spheres of its different departments, and mapping out the field of knowledge between them; while, by insisting on the importance as a preliminary to them all of a study of the general conditions under which proof in any department is to be reached, and of such methods of inquiry as can be employed in all, he became the founder of the system of logic which formed for many centuries the basis of philosophical instruction in Europe.

His detailed examination of one very common type of reasoning or inference gave it a place in the tradition of the schools as the pattern of all sound reasoning to which it may be questioned whether it was really entitled. This was what is known as the Syllogism; as an example of which, in the form considered by Aristotle as the most perfect, we may give this: 'Beings which can reason, and they only, are capable of a sense of humour; human beings, and they only, can reason; therefore human beings, and they only, are capable of a sense of humour.' But there are many sorts of syllogism beside this, in which the structure of the argument is the same, but which fall short of this in the completeness of correspondence which exists between the 'subjects' and the 'predicates' of the propositions concerned. The Syllogism is a form of argument, we may note, naturally assumed by discussion, such as the quick-witted talkers of Athens practised as a sort of game, in which one man made another admit two statements, and then produced a consequence, which would follow from putting the two together, but which the other disputant might not otherwise have been desirous of drawing. A dishonest player of this game might equivocate with a term of ambiguous meaning, or might in a long argument shift his ground undetected; it was such tricks as these that Aristotle exposed and classified in the list of 'fallacies' which has held its ground in manuals of logic until to-day.

Owing to the predominant influence exercised by Aristotle over the minds of thinking men in Europe during the Middle Ages, the source of the greater part of our philosophical, and of a large part of our scientific vocabulary is to be sought in the terms which he used. When we call the study of the ultimate nature of things *metaphysics*, we give it the name borne by the books in which he dealt with it because in the collected edition of his works they came 'after the *Physics*'. Even such familiar words as *habit*, *predicament*, *quality*, *accident*, and a vast number of others, which have passed from the language of the schools into that of daily life, are originally translations of technical expressions which occur in his writings.

In a picturesque passage, Bacon has observed that, 'when the Roman empire was overwhelmed by the deluge of the barbarian invasions, and human learning suffered shipwreck, the philosophies of Aristotle and Plato, like planks of lighter and less solid wood, were preserved amid the waves of time' which submerged the more weighty works of other Greek philosophers. Of these lost works, he probably had chiefly in mind those of the Atomists. The most celebrated of these, Democritus of Abdera, was a younger contemporary of Socrates. Like Plato, he held the eternal and ultimate reality in the world to be the object not of the senses, but of the understanding. But he conceived the nature of this reality very differently from Plato. It consisted of *atoms*, that is, of indivisible (and therefore indestructible) bodies, of a size too small to be detected by our senses, differing from one another in shape (whence he could call them by the same name as Plato gave to *his* ultimate realities, of 'Ideas' or 'Forms'), moving about in a vacuum or void. We remember that the Eleatics, holding the existence of a vacuum to be inconceivable, were led to deny the reality of motion, since this seemed impossible without a vacuum, and so cut themselves off from the possibility of giving any account of the various changes and processes which constitute the course of nature, except that of declaring them illusory.

The history of natural science in modern times has shown, on the other hand, that a theory which supposes such units of matter as Democritus called atoms (whatever difficulty the notion of a really indivisible unit of matter may involve) is of the greatest utility as an instrument for describing a vast number of physical processes in terms of the mutual combination and separation of such units, which are regarded as themselves remaining unchanged throughout. It was unquestionably a hindrance to the progress of natural science that the great influence of Aristotle, notwithstanding the respect which he felt for the learning and thoroughness of Democritus, was cast into the scale against the adoption of such a theory. But atomism seemed to him to stand condemned by its refusal to take the 'teleological' point of view, that is, to seek the deepest explanation of natural phenomena in the tendency of everything in nature towards the realization of the best and most perfect state of which it is capable. It was just on this account that Bacon preferred its method to that of Aristotle. While agreeing with Aristotle in condemning its blindness to the evidence of design in the world afforded by the existence of structures too elaborate ever to be explained satisfactorily by a 'fortuitous concourse of atoms', he was keenly sensible of the danger which lay in attempts to start in our investigations from a consideration of the purposes of nature, of which we are but too likely to take very shortsighted views. The English philosopher's preference of the Atomists to Aristotle in this respect no doubt gave encouragement to the subsequent fruitful revival of their hypothesis by students of natural science.

In antiquity, however, neither Plato nor Aristotle, who were the greatest thinkers of the age which immediately succeeded that of Democritus, did justice to the possibilities of atomism. The two hundred years which followed the death of Aristotle were years of great progress in mathematical and astronomical science. They were made illustrious by such names as those of Euclid, whose *Elements* was the textbook of geometry for two thousand years, of Eratosthenes, who first used the method by which the size of the earth is ascertained, of Archimedes, the discoverer of the principle of the lever, of Hipparchus, who has been called the true father of astronomy. But the researches of these great men lay in fields in which the help of the atomic theory of matter was not urgently needed. There was, indeed, a philosophical school which, during the period in question, adopted it as a fundamental part of their system. Its attraction to this school, however, was not its scientific utility so much as its apparent inconsistency with the doctrine of the divine government of the world, which they regarded as the source of the worst evil that affects mankind, namely the fear of death and of what may come after it. In more modern times, no doubt, scientific men have combined a belief in the atomic constitution of matter with a belief in divine government, but then they have held the atoms to be (as one of them—James Clerk Maxwell—put it) 'manufactured articles', and the world to include immaterial beings, which were not composed of atoms at all. The ancient Atomists, on the other hand, held the atoms to be eternal and nothing to exist that was not an assemblage of atoms, except the void in which the atoms moved. The school to whose adoption of atomism as a remedy against the terrors of religion I have referred was the Epicurean.

The name of Epicurean very early became a synonym for sensualist; but this was rather because sensualists could claim for their lives the sanction of the Epicurean principle that pleasure is the chief good, at which alone it is reasonable to aim, than because either the founder of the school (Epicurus, b. 341, d. 270)— whose personal character and teaching won the respect even of professed opponents of his philosophy—or his chief followers recommended by precept or example a life of sensual self-indulgence as the best means of attaining their goal. It cannot, indeed, be denied that, speaking generally, that man would be likely to secure for himself the greatest amount of pleasure and the least amount of pain who, like Epicurus himself, should live temperately and with dignity, surrounded by sympathetic friends, avoiding entanglement in harassing duties or exacting studies, and dispensing with anxious apprehensions of a future state of existence. But it is also undeniable that against a man who should think that, under his special circumstances, his best chance of passing his allotted time pleasantly lay in a 'short and merry' life of debauch, it would be difficult for a consistent Epicurean to maintain the superior advantages for such a person of what the world is agreed to regard as a more virtuous course.

The Epicurean school was confronted from its cradle by another, founded like itself at the end of the fourth century B.C., and known, not by the name of its founder Zeno, but by that of the Painted *Stoa* or Porch in Athens where he was accustomed to teach. This school opposed to the doctrine that the chief good was pleasure the doctrine that it was virtue. These two sharply contrasted doctrines continued for many centuries to divide the allegiance of a majority of thoughtful men in the countries which, at the beginning of the Christian era, formed the heart of the Roman empire. It will be remembered that the philosophers whom the Apostle Paul is related (Acts xvii. 18) to have encountered on his visit to Athens were representatives of the Epicureans and Stoics. With both schools, the central interest was not so much (as with most of the thinkers with whom we have hitherto been concerned) the attainment of the ultimate truth about the universe, as the discovery of the kind of life capable of best satisfying the individual's aspirations after happiness. The Stoics, who were wont to describe the best life as a 'life according to nature', set, indeed, a high value on the knowledge of the universal order, wherein an immutable destiny, or rather divine providence, had assigned to each of us a place, in the devout and cheerful acceptance of which lay the true secret of serenity among the changes and chances incident thereto. But, even so, intellectual or scientific activity is deposed from the place which it enjoyed in the estimation of a Plato or an Aristotle to the rank of an instrument of moral elevation; while to a consistent Epicurean—except so far as it served to dissipate the superstitious terrors, as man's deliverer from which the founder of his school seemed to the great Epicurean poet Lucretius (*b.* 96, *d.* 55) worthy himself to be called a god—it could hardly be more than a refined pastime.

We are thus not surprised to find that the Epicureans contributed little to the advance of scientific or philosophical inquiry. They adopted as their own the atomic theory of Democritus; but in their hands it was neither enabled to meet the objections which may be raised against it as a theory of the ultimate nature of reality, nor made to exhibit its great capacities as an instrument of scientific description and discovery. Nor yet can the Stoics, though some among them were eminent for their writings on certain branches of natural knowledge, be credited with any important advance in speculation, except on the subject of morality. In their theory of the world they attached themselves to Heraclitus, and the divine reason, which they held to be immanent in the world, 'reaching' like Wisdom in the *Wisdom of Solomon* (viii. 1) 'from one end to another mightily, and sweetly ordering all things', they conceived not as an immaterial spirit, but as of a fiery nature. Thus both schools, by identifying the real with the material, may be said to have fallen back from Plato, who had been the first clearly to distinguish the two conceptions. But the main interest of both schools lay, as we have seen, elsewhere, namely, in the problem of conduct. Nor was this wonderful, considering the circumstances of the period in which they flourished. The days of the old independent city-states of Greece were passing when Epicurus and Zeno taught; when St. Paul encountered their followers, the whole Greek world was already subject to the Roman emperors. Anxiety as to what one ought to do was bound to increase among men who had no longer to occupy them the obvious duties, administrative, military or judicial, which had in earlier days awaited as a matter of course the members of a small sovereign community like Athens in the time of Socrates.

Yet we have already seen that the teaching of this very Socrates, though himself a dutiful citizen, had in many cases tended to produce in his admirers a spirit of dissatisfaction with the traditional standards which, to their fellow-citizens, seemed bound up with the maintenance of the old civic loyalty. We find, too, that his example of a personal independence, secured by his refusal to entangle himself with the world by the pursuit of wealth or honours, inspired two remarkable men of his own generation, Aristippus and Antisthenes, with a zeal for the ideal of self-sufficient freedom for the individual, which carried them into one-sided exaggerations of their model. Two schools of philosophy thus took their rise. One was the Cyrenaic, taking its name from Aristippus' native city of Cyrene (in the modern Tripoli), which taught that men should live in the present, neither troubling themselves about the past, nor taking thought for the morrow, and not refusing any pleasure that came their way, so long as they were not brought under the power of it. The other, the school of Antisthenes, sought a like end rather by the opposite method of refusing whatever one could do without. Thus, its most celebrated member, Diogenes (of whose tub-dwelling every one has heard), dispensed even with a drinking cup when he had observed a boy drinking from the palm of his hand. This school was called the Cynic, from the Greek word for Dog, given as a nickname to Diogenes (d. 323), because of the shameless disregard for the conventions and even the decencies of life which his resolution to simplify his manner of existence to the uttermost led him to illustrate or defend. We still describe an ungenial contempt for popular sentiment as 'cynicism'.

Such principles as those of either Cyrenaic or Cynic were already out of tune with the old-fashioned feeling that the laws and customs of one's city belonged to the very substance of one's life; and it was a Cynic who first boasted that he was citizen of no particular city, but of the world—a 'cosmopolitan'. These two schools prepared the way for Epicureanism and Stoicism respectively; yet each continued its separate existence after the rise of the later systems. For neither was in all respects at one with its successor. The Epicurean's ideal was a life in which there was as little pain as possible, while the Cyrenaic stood ready to enjoy—though without surrendering himself to it— whatever pleasure any moment might bring. The Cynic and the Stoic both professed to live a life according to nature; but to the Cynic that was apt to seem natural which had in it the least trace of artifice, and therefore approached most nearly to the animal; while the Stoic gave the name to what reason showed to agree best with man's special place in nature, or even with the special place marked out for a particular man by the circumstances of a social position which was, after all, itself the appointment of destiny and of God.

Nothing, indeed, was more characteristic of the Stoics than their profound belief in such a divine apportionment of human lots. With them the claim to 'citizenship of the world', which they, like the Cynics before them, made for themselves, became no mere refusal to acknowledge any narrower citizenship, but the expression of a genuine conviction that the universe could claim from those of its inhabitants who were capable of apprehending and rejoicing in its wonderful order a loyal devotion at least as real as that which the patriot entertains for the imperfect institutions of his native land. 'The poet', cries the Stoic emperor Marcus Aurelius, 'can address Athens as "Thou dear city of Cecrops"; canst thou not address the Universe as "Thou dear city of God"?' It was not surprising that the Stoic was, of all the Greek schools, the one which made itself most at home among the Romans, who in less than two centuries after the death of the founder of that school had become masters of the Greek-speaking world. Love of knowledge and delight in beauty, the indulgence of subtle doubts and the cultivation of refined pleasures, were all alike un-congenial to the Roman temper. This was inclined to charge their representatives among Greek pro-fessors of philosophy with a frivolity dangerous to the sense of discipline and public duty, which had hitherto been the mainstay of the Roman state. But such suspicions were less aroused by the Stoics than by any of their rivals. Regarding the world as a commonwealth under the sovereignty of God, wherein every man was bound to subordinate his private interest to that of the whole, they took a view of life very consonant with the best Roman tradition; while their deep sense of a divine power, everywhere present, disposed them not only readily to conform to estab-lished religious customs, but to give to them, where possible, an interpretation consistent with their own philosophy. Thus in a world wherein, according to the Stoics (as to many modern men of science), the whole course of events is rigidly determined or pre-destined, it might well be that nothing could be otherwise than it is without a corresponding change in everything else. Hence there would be nothing incredible in a specially enlightened mind being able to infer, as the old diviners professed to do, from the state of the entrails of a sacrificed animal, the event of a battle which had not yet been fought. But if the moral and religious temper of Stoicism thus won it a special welcome at Rome, there was also something in the temper of the Roman people which was peculiarly congenial to the Stoic philosophy. This was what has been well called [1] 'the sense of justice and law, which marked out the Roman people among all the nations of antiquity, and which made the Roman legal system the basis on which the stability of society has ever since been built'. To the Stoics, the thought was already familiar of a law of nature by which all rational beings were bound, because it was the expression of the all-pervading reason which was God. They found in the Roman Law a material worthy of the attempt to mould it after this divine pattern, and the development of that law owed much to jurists who drew their inspiration thence.

The only philosophers of the Stoic school of whose teaching a record has descended to us in other than a fragmentary state, are representative of the later or Roman Stoicism. These are Seneca, Epictetus, and Marcus Aurelius. The first and third of these were in close touch with public affairs; for Seneca (b. A.D. 3, d. 65) during the earlier years of the reign of his pupil, Nero, was one of his chief advisers, while Marcus

[1] Professor P. Gardner, *The Growth of Christianity*, p. 163.

Aurelius actually occupied for twenty years (A.D. 161–180) the imperial throne. Epictetus, on the other hand, whose life spans the interval between those of the other two, was a slave. Marcus Aurelius himself counts his introduction to the discourses of Epictetus among the things in his life for which he had most cause to be grateful; and from these two men, in outward circumstances so unlike but spiritually very near akin, a multitude of thoughtful men in later generations have drawn strength and consolation in facing the battle of life. Both slave and monarch were beyond doubt of that 'small transfigured band' of which Matthew Arnold[1] speaks—

> Whose one bond is that all have been
> Unspotted by the world.

Neither the record of his life, nor the more self-conscious, less transparently sincere tone of his writings, enables us to say as much of Seneca. Yet few of the great writers of antiquity have done more than he to mould the moral sentiment of modern Europe; and, now that he is no longer so much studied at first hand as he was in the Middle Ages and in the period which followed the Renaissance, it would surprise many to discover how powerfully his influence, direct or indirect, has affected European literature. To him must be traced the tradition of a kind of moralizing, of which the consolations addressed in Shakespeare's *Measure for Measure* by the disguised Duke to Claudio in prison may serve as an example. Here a man is reconciled to death by insistence on the little satisfaction which can be got out of life. If we wonder

[1] *Stanzas in Memory of the Author of 'Obermann'.*

that neither the Duke nor Claudio, nor perhaps their creator, seems to look for anything more from a Christian priest (for as such the Duke is disguised), it is to be remembered that what may be called the conventional Christianity of educated men owes more than is always acknowledged to the Stoicism of Seneca. To the same source we owe the popular notion of a philosopher which is implied when we speak of 'bearing things philosophically', or when Shakespeare [1] says—

> There was never yet philosopher
> That could endure the toothache patiently,
> However they have writ the style of gods
> And made a push at chance and sufferance.

For the Stoics, Seneca among them, did not shrink from suggesting that only in the longer continuance of his wisdom and goodness had God the advantage over a truly wise and good man. Here, however in other respects the teaching of Stoicism could be confounded with that of Christianity, the divergence of the two religions (for Stoicism—at least in its later development—was a religion) might seem to be sufficiently obvious. Yet we must bear in mind that the Stoic who used such language would have admitted that of wise and good men in this high sense there had been very few or none; while the Christian, affirming that one such there had been, also affirmed that he was God.

I have just said that Stoicism was, or became, a religion, and have brought it into comparison and contrast with Christianity. We have, in fact, reached a period in the history of philosophy in which men

[1] *Much Ado About Nothing*, v. i. 35.

came to demand of philosophy that it should provide them with a religion, or, if it could not do this, should stand aside, and let religion provide them with a philosophy. To understand this period, we must now turn to the consideration of the mutual relations of Religion and Philosophy.

CHAPTER IV

PHILOSOPHY AND THE RISE OF CHRISTIANITY

WHEN men have begun to put to themselves questions of the kind in attempting to answer which philosophy consists, and to ask what is the true nature of this mysterious world in which they find themselves, how does it come to be there, and what is at the back of it all, they have never approached these inquiries with a mind completely free from prepossessions. In a far distant past their fathers had begun dimly to feel the presence of the mystery which encompassed them on every side. With a fearful sense of its strangeness to them, its weirdness and uncanniness, there was mingled an anticipation of the possibility of establishing a familiarity or of proving a kinship with it, wherein might lie the hope of a securer, freer, more powerful existence for themselves than was possible under other conditions. During a long course of ages, such fear of the mystery and desire of coming to terms with it, in combination with the more disinterested emotions of awe and curiosity, had everywhere given rise to some complicated system of forbearances and actions, of ceremonies and stories, expression of the habitual attitude of a people towards the powers that surround them and whose ways are not as theirs—in a word, to a religion.

Thus the philosopher, when he begins to philosophize, is already accustomed to a certain way of approaching the riddle which he desires to solve, by which he cannot fail to be affected, whether or no he be himself inclined to take it for a clue in his own investigations. But it belongs to the very essence of philosophy that it should not so take anything for granted as to refuse to test and examine it before admitting it as true. And so neither the initiators of a new philosophical movement, nor an individual who is beginning philosophical studies for himself, can avoid in the first instance taking up an attitude of independence towards religious tradition, which, if the representatives of that tradition do not tolerate it, may easily pass into hostility. The opposition between philosophy and religion, which we so frequently observe, is thus both natural and inevitable. It arises from the fact that they are both concerned with the same object. It does not, however, follow that philosophy must eventually take the place of religion as a better way of doing what religion has tried to do in an inferior manner. This might be so if the theories of the origin and course of nature which often form part of a religious tradition constituted the whole or the most important part of religion. But this is not so. Rather it would seem that men do not cease to find in the universe that which evokes and 'in divers portions and divers manners' satisfies their instinct of reverence, their impulse to worship. This experience can only find expression in some sort of religion. But, just because a religion is a response to what is felt to be the innermost heart of reality as a whole, .he whole nature of man necessarily claims to take part in it. Hence a religion, when once the level of spiritual development is reached at which philosophy can come into existence, can no more ignore or evade the criticism of philosophy, without abdicating its claim to express the response of the whole man to the divine, than philosophy in its turn can without self-mutilation ignore the testimony of religious experience to the nature of that ultimate reality which it seeks to apprehend as it truly is.

Now Greek philosophy in its earlier stages exhibits, on the whole, a remarkable independence of religious tradition. Nor, during the century which elapsed from the time of Thales to that of Anaxagoras, do we hear much of opposition to philosophy on the part of the representatives of religion. This may be accounted for by several considerations. There was no powerful priesthood, whose interest lay in maintaining existing opinions unchanged. There was no sacred book, generally accepted as containing doctrine necessary for salvation, with the statements of which the teachings of the philosophers could come into conflict. The very remoteness of the philosophers' speculations from the popular stories about the gods, and their indifference to the popular ritual which they probably had no desire to mend or end, would also tell against an outbreak of religious persecution. From the middle of the fifth to the middle of the fourth century B.C., a single Greek commonwealth, the democracy of Athens, was responsible for three celebrated acts of intolerance: the banishment of Anaxagoras for blaspheming the sun and moon, the execution of Socrates, and the indictment of Aristotle for impiety, which caused the philosopher to remove from Athens 'lest', as he is reported to have said, 'she should sin again against philosophy'. But in all these cases it is certain that there were at work other causes of animosity than the religious; and that personages disliked on political grounds were struck at through philosophers known to belong to their circle. Nor did these outbreaks of hostility to freedom of thought succeed in impairing the independence of philosophy.

We have already seen that, in the original Pythagoreanism, a scientific and philosophical movement was combined with a religious revival—and a revival, it would seem, not only of zeal in the worship of the divine powers, but along with this, of some very old notions and practices which we might think more at home among savages than among cultivated Greeks. These the later Pythagoreans dropped, or explained away as merely figurative or symbolical. But the religious strain was never lost in the Pythagorean school. We see this in the interest taken by it in the destiny of individual souls; an interest which it shared with, and probably derived from, the religious societies which regarded the writings ascribed to Orpheus as a divine revelation. It was the recognition of a religious need of the individual—however superstitious the rites by which they essayed to meet it—that gave these societies an advantage, in an age in which men were coming to think and feel for themselves, over the old state religions; for in those it was, one may say, only as a member of the State, or of some community which formed a recognized factor in it, that any one had a right or a duty to approach the higher powers. In the same way it is to the recognition of a religious need of the individual (and not to curiosity as to the philosophical problem of individuality) that is due the Pythagorean interest in individual souls, which expressed itself in the doctrine of their transmigration from body to body, and in which the Pythagoreans stand in marked contrast with the Ionian philosophers, to whose view of the world, based as it was on a purely scientific study of nature, the thought of a privilege exempting the souls of men from the universal law of change and decay was quite uncongenial.

The existence of Orphicism and of Pythagoreanism are sufficient evidence that anxiety about the salvation of one's soul was not unknown among the Greeks, or even among Greek philosophers, of what we are accustomed to call the classical period. But it becomes a far more prominent feature in the period which extends from the death of Aristotle and the conquests of his pupil Alexander in the fourth century before Christ to the establishment of Christianity as the religion of the Roman empire in the fourth century after Christ. This period is often called Hellenistic, because in it we have to do less with men born Hellenes or Greeks than with men of other nations and races who are Hellenizing. or playing the Greek; reading Greek, talking Greek, writing Greek, practising Greek customs, and following up the suggestions of Greek thinkers. Such men would bring with them to the work of carrying on the tradition of Greek civilization a temper far removed from the spirit which had, on the whole, characterized the older Greek philosophy; from its common sense and self-reliance, its scientific curiosity, and what in the phraseology of modern critics we may call its realism. After all, it is only to a minority that anywhere, even in ancient Greece, philosophy in what we are now apt to consider to be its proper sense, philosophy, that is, intent merely on understanding what things are, can be expected to

appeal. With a wider public came inevitably a
demand for something more than this could offer;
for some more practical response to those

> fifty hopes and fears
> As old and new at once as human life,

of which Browning [1] speaks as wont

> just when we are safest

in our own judgement from all such anxieties—morbid
anxieties, as they often seem in the eyes of those who
are exempt from them—

> To rap and knock and enter in our soul.

The age of which we are speaking had detached men
from their old moorings in small communities, where
the performance of accustomed duties left little room
for the question 'What must I do to be saved?' It had
launched them on the ocean of a world ringing with
contending voices, none of which spoke with an
authority that inspired unquestioning confidence. If,
from one point of view, it was an age marked (as an
eminent scholar [2] has lately put it) by 'failure of nerve',
this was the other side of a new sensitiveness to the
war of good and evil in the world, which, as the greatest
of the Greek philosophers, Plato, had shown, is as it
were focused in the human soul, and of a keener consciousness of the individual personality, which comes
to itself only in and through the struggle to maintain
itself against disruption in this intestine conflict. In
such an age we shall not be surprised to find a new
emphasis beginning to be laid on the hitherto far less

[1] *Bishop Blougram's Apology.*
[2] J. B. Bury, quoted in Gilbert Murray's *Four Stages of
Greek Religion*, p. 8.

prominent question of the freedom of the individual human will. The Epicureans and the Stoics espoused opposite sides on this question, the Epicureans maintaining that the will was free, the Stoics that it was determined. This may at first excite surprise; for we are nowadays inclined to connect the cause of religion with that of the freedom of the will; and the Stoics were the champions of religion against the Epicureans. But we must recollect, on the one hand, that with the Stoics the immutable order of nature which is often supposed to exclude the freedom of the will was identified with divine providence; and also that it is by no means the fact that the most deeply religious minds are those which dwell most readily on the thought of their own freedom to work out their own salvation. More often they are filled with a strong sense of their own individual helplessness and disposed to ascribe all the good that they do to the grace of God that is with them.

The central question in the philosophies of this period is that of the *end* at which a man should aim. Aristotle had, it is true, already stated in this form the problem of ethics; but ethics were with him rather an outlying province of philosophy than, as with the Stoics and Epicureans, its very heart. We cannot wonder that, side by side with these two great schools, each of which offered what seemed to be a definite answer to this question, is found a strong tendency to what is called Scepticism, the doubt whether a solution of this or any other ultimate problem is within our reach. Of this tendency Plato's college, the Academy, became the especial home. That the Stoics, rather than either the Epicureans or the Sceptics, exercised in the long run the widest influence in an age which was seeking for a religious faith, is to be explained by their attitude of devout acquiescence in the predestined or providential order of the universe. This religious strain in Stoicism is conspicuous throughout its history. We find it in the hymn of Cleanthes, the converted pugilist who succeeded the founder at the head of the school: 'Lead me, O Zeus, and thou, O Destiny, whithersoever I am appointed by you to go. Grant that I may follow without shrinking; but though in my wickedness it should not be with my own good will, yet I must follow none the less.' And we find it no less, four centuries later, in the concluding words of Marcus Aurelius' *Meditations*: 'It is he who decreed thy fashioning that now decrees thy dissolution; thou art accountable neither for the one nor for the other; therefore depart in peace, as he that bids thee depart is at peace with thee.' But it is in the later Stoics, and more particularly in Seneca, that a profounder sense of human infirmity is observed to temper the severity characteristic of the school with a milder and more philanthropic spirit, and to give rise to a resemblance between his writings and those of his contemporary the Apostle Paul, with whom a legend, at least as old as the fourth century after Christ, represented him as having been on terms of friendship and correspondence. The existence of this legend helped, indeed, to win for Seneca an authoritative place among the teachers of a later time, when the faith of Paul had become the accepted religion of Europe.

In a history of philosophy it is not necessary to dwell upon the process by which, in an age characterized, as we have seen, by the general quest of a religion more satisfactory intellectually, morally, and emotionally than any of those hitherto acknowledged by the inheritors of the Greek civilization, a period of struggle among numerous competitors ended in the victory of Christianity. But so great has been the influence of Christianity upon the later history of European thought, that something must be said of the relation between the doctrines of this religion and those of the philosophical schools which were flourishing when it first appeared, as well as of any contribution which it may be thought to have made to the stock of problems requiring philosophical discussion, or of conceptions capable of use in philosophical inquiry.

The Jewish nation, in the midst of which Christianity arose, had come under the guidance of its prophets to see in their own god the one only God, beside whom was no other, and in the whole frame of nature the work of his hands, which he had wrought in wisdom and righteousness. The Greeks, under the guidance of philosophers like Plato and the Stoics, had also come to recognize the unity of the divine nature, and to trace in the order of the world a divine wisdom and justice. But the Greek philosophers, in thus eliminating from their own theology the unworthy and superstitious elements of popular religion, had been at little pains to purify the popular religion itself. Before the days of the Stoics, they had usually left it on one side with contemptuous tolerance; and even the Stoics did not endeavour so much to reform it as to find even in its most repulsive features a harmless symbolism. The occasional use of the name Zeus for the divinity is almost the only obvious link between Greek philosophical theology and the religious traditions of the nation. Even the veneration of the heavenly bodies commended itself to Plato and Aristotle rather as being part of the religion of all nations than as belonging specially to that of their own. The Jewish prophets, on the other hand, had—partly, no doubt, because they were prophets, and not philosophers—been deeply concerned to connect their theology with the religion of their fellow countrymen. Their one God of all the earth is still the God of Israel; the traditional worship of Israel is to become, as far as may be, worthy of his perfect righteousness.

Christianity here was true to the principles of the prophets. Jesus himself 'came not to destroy, but to fulfil'; and Paul, though he broke with the Jewish community and its law, had no thought of connecting what was now plainly a new religion with any other but that which had been his own. The Christians, whether Jews or Gentiles, were to succeed to the privileges of the old Israel, and to offer to the God who was now ready to admit all men to covenant with himself a worship in spirit, though not in form, the same as Israel had offered to him when Israel alone of all peoples had possessed a genuine knowledge of his will. Christianity thus combined a conception of God comparable in elevation to that reached by the Greek philosophers with the offer of a fellowship, not merely in a philosophical school, but in a religious body of initiated brethren. Such bodies were at that time well known in connexion with all manner of worships, Egyptian, Syrian, and Persian, which were competing for the allegiance of seekers after a closer intercourse with God than the old established state religions pretended to give.

Even independently of, though contemporaneously with, the rise of Christianity, such Jewish writers as the Alexandrian Philo and the author of the *Wisdom of Solomon* had sought in the philosophies of Plato and of the Stoics a confirmation of their religious convictions, or even a key to the inner meaning of their sacred books. And it was with these same philosophies that Christianity showed itself most sympathetic. It was, indeed, ready to take its stand with philosophy in general against the current superstitions most offensive to a philosophic mind. Astrology and divination (which many even of the philosophers were prepared to defend) found no place in its system. Its worship was free from animal sacrifice, with its repulsive accompaniments, and from any traces of that obscenity which haunted at least the outskirts of so many other religions, and also, in the days of its primitive simplicity, from many sensuous attractions, as of images, incense and the like, which were in later ages adopted by the Church. These characteristics did not, indeed, distinguish Christian worship from that of the Jewish synagogues; but the new religion had laid aside the national prejudices of Judaism and its respect for the punctilious observance in daily life of a host of minute traditional regulations.

The Christian and the Stoic were at one, as against the Epicurean, in their exacting standards of conduct, and in their faith in the divine government of the world. Moreover, while the Epicureans saw in the course of nature an eternal play of atoms, without any predestined plot, the Stoics and the Christians alike looked forward to a conflagration in which the present frame of things would perish. But this conflagration was by the Stoics inferred from a particular physical theory; by the Christians it was expected as the predicted accompaniment of a great assize, in which a moral judgement was to be passed on the deeds of all men, and a new order introduced in which the good should be for ever happy, the wicked for ever miserable. For Christian beliefs about the destiny of the external world did not originate, like those of the Greek philosophers, in speculations prompted by scientific curiosity; they were accepted on authority, and justified as suitable to the character of a righteous ruler of the universe. Thus ethics were even more central in the view of the world taken by the early Christians than in the philosophy of the Stoics.

But the ethics of Christianity, however like to those of Stoicism so far as concerns the kind of conduct approved by both, differed from them in this, that it was not in his own strength that the Christian aimed at fulfilling the moral law; it was by the grace of Another. Like the Jew and the Stoic, he counted himself a child of God; not, however, in right of his nation like the Jew, nor in his own right like the Stoic, but in right of his adoption into the society of one who was God's son by nature. Here the consciousness of human infirmity, which at this period was vividly present even in a representative Stoic like Seneca, was met by the belief in the mediation of a divine Saviour. It was not, indeed, only among the Christians that we find at the time a belief of this kind. But nowhere else was the Saviour presented as 'come in the flesh' a few years since in the person of one who, although living in obscure and humble circumstances (but no humbler than those of Epictetus), and dying (by an unjust sentence, like Socrates) a criminal's death, had so lived, taught, and died, that even men whose ideal was found in such sages as I have just mentioned could, with the martyr Justin, who himself had passed to Christianity from the philosophical schools, recognize in him the supreme revelation of the divine Reason which had dwelt also in them.

It was this principle of mediation which formed a link between Christianity and Platonism. In one of the most difficult but most influential of his writings, the *Timaeus*, Plato had spoken of the world of eternal natures or Ideas as the model or pattern according to the likeness of which the visible world was created by God. In an age like that in which Christianity arose, haunted as it was by a sense of falling immeasurably short of a perfection after which it was at the same time passionately yearning, these expressions of Plato were taken as affording the highest philosophical sanction to the thought that there might be found some mediating power to bridge the gulf which was felt to yawn between God and man. The eternal pattern of the created world could be identified with that Word or Angel of Jahweh (Jehovah) of which the later Jewish piety had—in its reverent shrinking from the application of anthropomorphic language to the supreme object of its worship—come to speak, rather than of Jahweh himself, when describing his communings with prophets and holy men of old, and which the Christians held to have become incarnate in Jesus.

In a celebrated passage of his *Confessions*[1] the great Christian writer Augustine, of whom we shall have to speak again, tells us that he had learned from

[1] Book VII. c. 9.

the Platonists the same doctrine as was taught also in the opening verses of the Fourth Gospel about the eternal Word of God, himself God, the immediate agent in the creation of the world, the light and life of men; but not the doctrine of the following passage that this 'Word was made flesh and dwelt among us'. This observation illustrates the fact that, while the Platonism of his day (which we now call Neoplatonism, and of which we shall speak again) agreed with Christianity in teaching a doctrine of mediation, the two systems differed in that by this mediation the later Platonism aimed in the main at keeping a distance between the material world (to which our 'flesh' belongs) and the divine goodness, Christianity rather at bringing the divine goodness down into the very midst of that world. This was held to have been accomplished in the incarnation of the Word in the person of Jesus, who, according to the view which finally prevailed, was at once truly God and truly man, with a real human body and soul. Such a view was found to be capable, as others were not, of satisfying the requirements of the Christian's consciousness that, in virtue of union with Jesus through solemn incorporation in the society which lived by the power of his Spirit, he was actually reconciled to God. A supernatural being with a phantasmal body which could only seem to suffer and to die, or even with a real body but with no human feelings or affections, or again a being, whether man or more than man, who was not in a genuine sense one with the supreme God, would not have served his turn. Hence the rejection as 'heresies' of proposals to describe the nature of Jesus in any such terms. Moreover, the same considerations as made Christians shrink from anything which might weaken the connexion between the mediator and either of the two parties, God and man, which in him were to come together, excluded also the possibility of recognizing more mediators than one.

On the other hand, if we turn to the contemporary systems of partially christianized theosophy or religious speculation—which are usually grouped under the common name of Gnosticism, because their adherents claimed for an inner ring of initiates the exclusive possession of a secret *gnosis*, that is, knowledge or wisdom—we find them indulging a mythological fancy in the invention of long chains of mediators between God and man. So, also, did the latest representatives of a Platonism that refused to come to terms with Christianity. These were actuated at once by the philosopher's desire to discover the structure of reality by distinguishing the different kinds of being, by the religious desire to remove the divine nature as far as might be from contact with matter, and by the controversial desire to justify against Christianity, the now dying paganism, in its recognition of a host of divine beings of various grades. This tendency to multiply mediators reacted on Christianity itself, practically in the development of saint-worship, and theoretically in the interpolation of a hierarchy of angels between a Christian and his Saviour, similar to the hierarchies of gods in the latest Platonism, by a writer who took the name of St. Paul's Athenian convert, Dionysius the Areopagite. In an uncritical age he acquired a high authority as a companion of the Apostle. But his angelic hierarchies, though they play an important part in the scheme of Dante's

Paradise, never became prominent objects of popular devotion; while the saints, who did, yet have never been openly held to intercept the direct access of the individual Christian to the one true Mediator Jesus Christ, or to possess the divine nature which, according to the Christian creed, is in him alone personally united with the human.

From the relation of Christianity to the philosophical schools of older origin, we may now turn to the contribution which it made to the stock of problems demanding philosophical discussion, and of conceptions capable of use in philosophical inquiry.

The philosophical problem which, in consequence of a deepening of the sense of individual personality through the religious experience gained under the influence of Christianity, assumes a new importance is that of personality in God and in man. The principal conceptions framed in the course of the effort to give expression to this religious experience, which have proved themselves of use also to philosophers, are those of a triune God and of divine grace.

In deepening the sense of individual personality, Christianity did but carry forward a process which we have already seen to be characteristic of the age in which it arose. But Christianity was especially qualified to carry it forward because the religious experience of the Christian was pre-eminently an experience of personal intercourse with a personal God. For, in the first place, he inherited the Jewish faith that God was one, not merely in the sense that all the various powers and influences which seem to be active in nature are somehow manifestations of a single energy or life, but rather in the sense in which we recognize in the various acts of a human being the unity of a moral character. In the second place, he was not left to mere speculation in framing for himself a definite conception of the divine character; he was referred for this purpose to the historical character of Jesus as represented in the traditional records of his life and teaching. In the third place, according to that teaching as so recorded, it was in the personal service of other men, especially of the members of the Christian brotherhood, that personal intercourse with Jesus was to be realized: 'Inasmuch as ye did it unto one of these my brethren, even these least, ye did it unto me' (Matt. xxv. 40).

As soon as intellectual curiosity is aroused in regard to this kind of religious experience, it must inevitably fasten upon the question: What must be the nature of God and of man, and of the mediator between them, for such intercourse to be possible?

Such questions, once stirred, appealed to other passions than intellectual curiosity, and the controversies which they occasioned can scarcely be said to belong to the history of philosophy; but the results of these controversies cannot be excluded from it. For these results, embodying, as on the whole they did, the judgement passed in the long run by the common sense of the Christian community on the various attempts to think out the problems involved, came to constitute a body of doctrine which, during the period in which Christianity has been the dominant religion of Europe, could not but be present to the thoughts of those who were engaged in further investigation of the same questions.

Although this whole group of questions concerned

the mutual relations of God and man, attention was at first concentrated on those which concerned primarily the divine nature, and asked: In what sense and how far is the mediator (who is certainly man) to be considered as God? Afterwards came the turn of those which, starting from the other side, inquired: In what sense and how far can a man, when he does God's will (which he can certainly only do by the help of God's grace), claim any merit therein for himself?

The questions which were thus raised among Christian theologians in the third and fourth centuries of our era respecting the divine nature were also being discussed at the same time, in independence of the special doctrines of Christianity, by the philosophers of whom mention has already been made as being in the estimation of their contemporaries Platonists, but whom modern critics, perceiving a considerable difference between their doctrines and those of Plato, call Neoplatonists. To them, as to the Christian thinkers of their time, the philosophical questions suggested by religion were of primary importance; while those suggested by the natural sciences, which turned away from what was above man to what was below him, from that to which he was allied through his spiritual nature to that to which he was allied through his body, were practically negligible. The greatest of the Neoplatonists was Plotinus, who lived in the third century. In his speculations on the nature of the highest reality, in apprehending and uniting itself with which (so far as possible) the human soul might expect to find its noblest aspirations satisfied, Plotinus carried on the speculations of those older Greek philosophers who had not, like the Epicureans, refused

altogether to see in the world the manifestation of a
spiritual or divine principle.   Such philosophers were
the Stoics, who had acknowledged as present everywhere in the world the operation of a divine providence.
Such was Aristotle, who had explained the motion of
the universe by its attraction towards a supreme
Intelligence which, in the activity of contemplating
its own most excellent nature, enjoyed an eternal and
self-sufficing life of bliss.   Such, above all, was Plato,
who, in the very fact that the eternal natures of things
could be apprehended by our intelligence, recognized
the presence of a principle of order to which it was
due that these natures were what the intelligence
apprehends them as being, and also that the intelligence
apprehends them as being what they are.   The same
Plato, in a passage of his *Timaeus* to which reference has
already been made, had spoken not only of this supreme
principle, but of the world of Ideas or eternal natures,
as an eternal living being, the pattern of the world
which our senses perceive; he had also spoken of a
soul, made in the likeness of this being, as that which
gives unity and motion to this same sensible world.

In this triad or trinity of beings, all of which might
be called divine, the second corresponds to the Intelligence of which Aristotle had spoken as though it were
the highest of all, the third to that all-pervading Life
of the world which was the chief God of the Stoics.
To the eternal Intelligence Plotinus did not, like
Aristotle, deny as unworthy of its dignity the contemplation of natures other than its own; or rather its own
nature includes for Plotinus the natures of all other
things, which are related to it not as objects external
to it, but as the thoughts the thinking of which makes

up its own life. But the spiritual ambition of Plotinus was not to be satisfied by sympathy with the universal Life, nor yet by contemplation of the eternal Intelligence. He sought, and was believed by his friends on several occasions to have attained, a union with the ultimate principle, the highest God of all. Now the Highest must, according to him, be above all distinction whatever, even that of the knower from the known, which remains with the most exalted Intelligence, although in its case what knows and what is known are the same being, making itself, as it were, into two in order to have self-knowledge. Hence union with the Highest can be attained only in a state in which all sense of distinction is lost, a state of ecstasy or rapture. Here Plotinus speaks a different language from Plato. Plato had acknowledged that, in the correspondence of intelligence to reality which takes place in knowledge, there was revealed an underlying principle of unity which could neither be called Intelligence as opposed to Reality, nor Reality as contrasted with Intelligence. But there is no proof that he supposed this underlying principle to be revealed except just in this way. When he speaks of experiences like rapture or ecstasy, he ranks them below the experience of the philosopher, who thinks out what in such experiences is only, as it were, seen in a glass darkly. In giving to such experiences, in which thought is not active, a higher rank than to thought, Plotinus shows himself to be what Plato is often called, but, strictly speaking, is not, namely a *mystic*. Such mysticism is an indication that we have in Plotinus one who is working out the extreme consequences of that concentration of interest on the spiritual life of the individual which we have seen to be characteristic of the thought of the early centuries of our era. No less social ideal has ever been put forward than that of the ardent lover of God who casts aside one lesser good after another, which he finds not to be the one original and supreme goodness, until, unencumbered by anything that can distract him from the object of his quest, he takes his flight, in the words of Plotinus himself, 'alone to the Alone'. Yet it must not be forgotten that it is not in the true interest of society that the individuality of its members should not be developed to the full; and, in the long run, it reaps advantage from the loneliest of spiritual adventures. Through the religious passion for an individual access to God, which is the driving force behind the philosophical mysticism of Plotinus, the individual learns to claim for himself a unique value and place in the universe. That of every individual man, and not only of the human species, there is a distinct eternal nature, 'Form', or 'Idea', is expressly taught by Plotinus, as it had not been by Plato or by Aristotle.

But with Plotinus only the first member of his Trinity is God in the highest and fullest sense. The second and third are emanations from the supreme Godhead, through whose intervention it can, without coming into direct contact with matter, produce therein a reflection of its goodness, namely, the order and beauty of the visible world. Thus only can the soul capable of the mystic rapture unite itself with the veritable God; and the virtues of social life are merely the lowest rungs of the ladder by which the heavenward ascent is made. The view eventually developed by the

Christian theologians is different. In Jesus himself, and in the Spirit which is active in the common life of the Christian Church, and so in social fellowship or love, they recognized manifestations of eternal and necessary elements in the supreme Godhead. With such a view, it becomes possible, in the first place, to conceive the supreme Godhead not as a bare unity without any distinctions within it (such as no real unity within our experience can well be said to be), but as a unity of distinct elements, the distinctness of which is as necessary to their unity as their unity to the full realization of their distinct characteristics; in other words, as a unity of the kind whose most obvious type is to be found in love. In the second place, not only to the philosopher and the ecstatic saint, but to all believers in Jesus and sharers in his Spirit, and so to the humblest members of the Christian community, is secured a direct access to the supreme Godhead. Lastly, in the human life of Jesus the supreme Godhead is regarded as in direct contact with the material world. This account of the divine nature may be, I think, shown to be philosophically (as well as religiously) superior to that given by Plotinus. The representation of the supreme Godhead as accessible to all men, and as in contact with the material world, harmonizes with a philosophy which allows to the facts of history and of nature a significance in the scheme of things which for Plotinus they could scarcely possess. Such a philosophy will be more in accord than that of Plotinus with the spirit of Plato, who makes Parmenides, in the Dialogue which bears his name, tell the youthful Socrates that a reluctance to allow the existence of Ideas or eternal natures corresponding to things we consider mean and contemptible is a sign of philosophical immaturity.

The representation of the supreme Godhead as itself a trinity, and not merely as the highest member of a trinity, has still greater philosophical importance. Even thinkers of the greatest genius both in ancient and in modern times have found it hard to succeed in describing the unity of any group of things, and still more the unity of the whole of reality, without speaking of it as though the differences within it were somehow unreal and, if we saw things as they were, would disappear altogether. Moreover, in escaping this pitfall, philosophers have often fallen into one on the other side of their path. They have spoken as though real things were all utterly separate and different from each other; and as though, when we talk of a class or kind, and still more of a world or universe, the unity were only in our minds, and not in the things at all. Nevertheless we know that we cannot speak of things as *many* without calling them at the same time *one*— they must be many apples, or many men, or at the least, many things. Why then call the many by one name, if there be no real unity among them? Yet whatever unity there be among them cannot be something over and above them, which can dispense with them; it must rather be constituted by them, many as they are.

No doubt there are groups in which each member of the group might seem easily dispensed with. For example, one grain more or less in a heap of sand matters little enough; but, just for that reason, the unity of the heap matters very little too. Divide it into two or three, and what harm is done? But divide an organism, a plant or animal, into two, and, unless it be done with discretion, the organism will die, will function as a plant or animal no more. And the higher in the scale of organic life it be, the less easy it is to divide it without injuring or even killing it. This is so just because, the higher it is, the less possible it is for one of the parts to take another's place. Some lowly animal organisms, if turned inside out, will, it is said, soon adapt themselves to the new state of things; a higher organism could not do this. The more thoroughly differentiated are the parts, the more intimately one is the whole. Moreover, if the parts were to be conscious of themselves and of their unity, we should think this a higher type of unity still; and, therefore, the unity of a society of human beings, though it is often precarious and unstable, seems to be a higher kind of unity than that of a body. If the members of a society were perfectly equal and yet so individually different that each was indispensable to the others, and if they were bound together by no constraint but that of love and of a love which was completely satisfied and reciprocated, this society would certainly seem to be the very ideal of a unity of many members. Now, it has certainly been a circumstance beneficial to philosophical thought in Europe that the received theology has ascribed just such a structure as this to the supreme Being; that it has not set up for worship a Unity beyond all distinctions, and therefore unknowable, but one to whose inmost nature it belongs to reveal itself in the very processes of knowledge and love by which the worshipper apprehends it.

We now come to those among the problems set by

the religious experience of Christians to Christian theologians which concern human responsibility. Here the movement of theological speculation did not result in an authoritative formula; and, therefore, no such clear statement of its outcome can be made as in the case of the doctrine of the nature of God. What most concerns the historian of philosophy is this: that the universal order, which the Christians agreed with the Stoics in regarding as divine, was by Christians viewed, in its relation to man, not so much in the character of destiny as in that of 'grace' or free favour. So long as men followed the Stoics in neglecting the advantages which theories like the atomism borrowed from Democritus by the Epicureans offered for a mechanical explanation of natural processes, and in looking upon morality as of vastly more importance in the universe than the motions of lifeless bodies, the distinction between the Stoic 'destiny' and the Christian 'purpose of grace' was, perhaps, of slight philosophical (though no doubt of much religious) importance. But it is otherwise when the success which has attended attempts at the mechanical explanation of natural phenomena, and the impression of human insignificance produced by the discovery that the earth is not the centre of the universe, have encouraged attempts to minimize the difference between voluntary activity and the movements of inanimate things, and even, in the interests of a comprehensive theory, to give the lie to our natural conviction that we act freely. To such attempts a consciousness of spiritual freedom trained in the tradition of a teaching which put 'grace' in the place of 'destiny' offers a stronger resistance than could have been expected from one trained under a system which preferred to use the latter term, and tended to be careless of the distinction of the spiritual from the material.

The question of the respective parts to be assigned in men's good actions to divine grace and to their own free will gave rise at the beginning of the fifth century after Christ to a controversy, which has since been many times renewed. At that time, the champions of free will and grace respectively were a monk named Pelagius, interesting as the first person of British blood to win fame as writer and thinker, and Augustine, who died A.D. 430 as bishop of Hippo in Africa, than whom few men have exercised a profounder influence over the intellectual and spiritual development of Europe. After a youth of 'storm and stress', of which he has left us an account in his *Confessions*, he had learned how deeply seated in the human heart are its inclinations to evil, and had become profoundly conscious of the need of divine grace to counteract them; and more than once in a later age, when a strong sense of sin and of moral helplessness has fallen upon men, they have given it expression by a revival of Augustine's teaching. His keen analysis of his own experience made him a pioneer—especially through his study of memory—in what is now called psychology. In him may be said to culminate that concentration of interest on the individual soul which we have seen to be characteristic of the period described in this chapter. He was greatly attracted and influenced by the mysticism of Plotinus, which, as we saw, exhibited this tendency in an extreme form; and his sympathetic references to the Platonism of his day helped much in keeping alive some knowledge of the Platonic philosophy through the dark days for European civilization which were now at hand. For already the inundation, of which Bacon speaks in a passage already quoted, in which the learning of the ancient world was to suffer shipwreck, had begun. As Augustine lay dying, the Vandals, whose name has become a proverb for destructive barbarism, were besieging his episcopal city. But he had already expressed, in his great work on the *City of God*, written after the sack of Rome by the Goths in 410, his conviction that not in the secular state of which Rome was the centre and symbol, and which seemed now to lie at the mercy of the invaders from the north, but in the Christian Church, which could boast more truly than Rome of being the 'eternal city', could the human spirit find an abiding home.

CHAPTER V

PHILOSOPHY DURING THE MINORITY OF MODERN EUROPE

THE century which followed the death of Augustine saw Rome itself under the government of barbarian chieftains. The greatest of these, Theodoric (who died A.D. 526), although himself illiterate, chose for his ministers two men, among the most cultivated that that age could boast, Cassiodorus and Boethius. These made it their business, being keenly alive to the dangers which at that time threatened the very tradition of the ancient civilization, to save what they could from the 'shipwreck of learning' for the times that should come after them. In the foundation by Cassiodorus, on his retirement in A.D. 540 from public life, of a society of monks provided with a large collection of books, and enjoined to spend a great part of their time in the study of them, we may see the beginnings of the custom by which institutions of this kind, into which men withdrew from the ordinary business of the world to live a life more strictly in accord with the principles of Christianity than they thought possible elsewhere, became the chief means by which classical literature escaped destruction.

The same scholar's tract on the Seven Liberal Arts was one of two or three works of this period which helped to fix the curriculum that was to dominate the ages we call 'Middle Ages', as lying between those we call without hesitation 'ancient' and those we call without hesitation 'modern'. Three of these arts were more elementary, and formed the *trivium* (whence our word 'trivial'), namely, Grammar, Logic, and Rhetoric; four (the *quadrivium*) more advanced, Arithmetic, Geometry, Astronomy, and Music. It was in these 'arts' that the degree in Arts at our old universities was originally given.

To Cassiodorus' friend and colleague Boethius the philosophy of the Middle Ages owed a more direct debt. Stripped, after years of prosperity, by an unjust charge of treason, of all his honours, and lying in a prison whence he was only to be brought out to die, he distilled, as it were, into a little book of meditations the teaching of Plato and the Stoics concerning the preferable state of the just sufferer to the prosperous sinner, and the duty of faith, amid all appearances to the contrary, in the perfection of the eternal and providential order of the universe. This *Consolation of Philosophy*, which he represents as administered to him by Philosophy in person, came, despite the absence from it of any reference to Christian beliefs—though it is probable that Boethius, while not, as the legend said, a Christian martyr, was a professing Christian—to be regarded in the Middle Ages almost as a sacred book; and it was the first of those which King Alfred chose to translate and expound for the instruction and edification of his rude West Saxon subjects. But it was not only the religious and practical teaching of the old philosophers which Boethius had much to do with passing on to the men of the Middle Ages. In his desire to promote among his contemporaries the knowledge of matters which were in imminent danger of being forgotten, he translated from Greek into Latin a large number of scientific writings, among them works of Plato, of Aristotle, of Euclid, and of Archimedes. Not all of them survived; but his versions of Aristotle's works on logic and his commentaries on them bore an important part in the philosophical education of the most active minds among the ancestors of the modern nations of Europe. Together with the treatises of Aristotle himself on the various kinds of judgement and of inference, he also translated and expounded at length a little work introductory to the most elementary of these, from the pen of a certain Porphyry, who had lived at the end of the fourth century, a friend and disciple of Plotinus, and a strong opponent of Christianity.

This work, which is a quite unpretending textbook, dealt with what were called the 'five predicables'. Porphyry's illustrations will explain this expression. If I say 'Socrates is a man', I state the kind or *species* of being that he is; if I say 'men are animals', the *genus* or kind of being that men—and many other things as well—are; if I say 'men are possessed of reason', the *difference* which marks off the human species from other species of the genus 'animal'. Again, if I say 'men are capable of a sense of humour', I state a *property* of human nature, a characteristic, that is, belonging to human beings only, and to them as human beings, which follows from that which distinguishes them from other animals, namely, their possession of reason. Lastly, if I say of any men that they are fair or dark or sitting down, I am mentioning *accidents* of human nature, characteristics which men may have or may not have, or states which they may or may not be in. Now, speaking at the very outset of this book of the first two of these predicables, *genus* and *species*, Porphyry observes that the question may be raised whether *genera* and *species* exist only in the mind or independently of it, whether they have a being apart from the individuals which belong to them or not. But these questions he passes by without deciding, as beyond the ken of so elementary a discussion as that upon which he is engaged. The passage, which at once called the attention of his readers to problems of far more interest and importance than the immediate subject of the book in which it occurred, is a good example of the way in which what is called elementary logic may attract attention to great philosophical problems. Especially did it serve this purpose in the days of the gradual intellectual revival which we may date from the return to western Europe under Charles the Great (crowned by the Pope as successor of the old Roman emperors on Christmas Day A.D. 800) of something more like a settled and civilized government than it had for some time enjoyed.

Such elementary logic is only concerned directly with classifying forms of statement and distinguishing ambiguities among them; but behind the study of these lie those questions about the relations of the 'one' to the 'many' with which we have met before, in connexion first with the philosophy of Socrates, Plato, and Aristotle, and again with the Christian theologians and their doctrine of the Trinity.

Porphyry tells us of *genera* and *species*: and we ask: 'How are many individuals all one species? And how are many species all one genus?' We are always coming up against this difficulty of reconciling the 'one' and the 'many'. The whole world of our experience is stamped, as it were, throughout and in every part, with the character of being 'one in many, and many in one'. Every generation of philosophers, in presence of freshly discovered facts or of old facts reconsidered, finds itself confronted with new forms of the old puzzle, in dealing with which it may learn from the history of philosophy to avoid old mistakes, and to profit by the insight of its predecessors.

The men of the earlier Middle Ages in western Europe were haunted by the sense that they were ignorant of much that a past age had known. They did not, perhaps, fully realize—though some of them were not without more than an inkling of it—that they were in the position of shipwrecked children. For their Christian training had accustomed them to think of books handed down from antiquity as the repository of divine revelation; and so it seemed natural to them to seek, as it were, for the necessaries and conveniences of the intellectual life among the scanty relics of the ancient literature, rather than to catch their own food and invent their own tools. The elementary logic of Aristotle (which was all that they had of his philosophy from the ninth to the twelfth century) was an ingenious tool in which the ablest scholars took much delight; through practising the use of it they sharpened their wits, and in the eleventh century some were beginning to venture on using it for the picking of locks with which the less bold among them thought it dangerous to tamper.

The great French, or rather Breton, logician and theologian, Peter Abelard (1079–1142), whose lectures on the Mont Ste.-Geneviève at Paris were the nucleus of the University which was afterwards the chief centre of intellectual activity in the west during the

Middle Ages, underwent much persecution at the hands of more conservative theologians—especially of the saintly mystic and ecclesiastical reformer, Bernard of Clairvaux (1091–1153). It seemed to them that he was irreverently bringing into the study of the most sacred subjects a reckless ambition to be victorious over antagonists in debate, in which the 'dialecticians' of the twelfth century after the Christian era resembled the sophists of the fourth century before it. His method of setting forth what could be said on different sides of every question, his delight in pitting one revered authority against another, his love of seeking in pagan writers instruction on religious subjects, were all, they thought, to be accounted for by his inability to lay aside, even in theology, the disputatious methods of logic and the excessive reverence for heathen masters which was natural in a professor of a science whose oracle was Aristotle. But the next generation of theologians had been Abelard's pupils; and before long the method of approaching every question by the stating of the arguments for and against a particular solution became the recognized method of the schools or lecture-rooms, the distinguishing mark of those whom we call the 'Schoolmen' and of their 'scholastic' philosophy.

In respect also of the other point which had been objected to Abelard did it turn out true that 'the heresy of one generation was the orthodoxy of the next'. The recovery in the twelfth and thirteenth centuries of the other works of Aristotle, besides those which dealt with the elementary logic on which he was already the recognized authority, provided the grateful scholars of that age with a teacher who seemed ready with an answer (if sometimes one of uncertain meaning) to every scientific and philosophical question that could be raised. It might have been possible for theology to have kept elementary logic at arm's length; but the newly found works of Aristotle were encyclopaedic in range, and plainly discordant in certain respects with the traditional teaching of the Christian Church. These disagreements were, moreover, emphasized by the fact that some of the most important books of Aristotle had come to western Europe through the Mahommedan scholars of Spain and accompanied by their comments thereon. One of these, in particular, Ibn Rosch, who was called in Latin Averroes (1126–98), came to be entitled *par excellence* 'the commentator', as Aristotle himself was 'the philosopher'. Averroes was a nominal Mahommedan, but Aristotle was the master whom he followed as an infallible guide; and two doctrines, in particular, which he found in his master's writings, those of the eternity of the world and the mortality of the individual human soul, were as inconsistent with the traditional teaching of the Mahommedan religion as with that of the Christian. It became an urgent demand that the learned world of western Europe should make up its mind as to the bearing of Aristotle's teaching on doctrines usually accepted as part of a divine revelation.

Of those who attempted to face the problem thus presented and work out a solution, the most celebrated is Thomas Aquinas (who died, while still under fifty, A.D. 1274), a Dominican friar, whose system of philosophical theology (which supplied much of the framework of Dante's *Divina Commedia*) was one of the greatest achievements of the Middle Ages. Herein he essayed to harmonize, so far as possible, the newly recovered speculations of Aristotle with the Christian view of the world. In doing this, he did not simply piece his authorities together; he thought out for himself each point as it came up, and produced, despite the impediments to the free play of speculative thought which constant deference to various authorities demanded, a masterpiece of sober criticism and of keen insight into the genuine significance and affinities of the positions adopted or rejected. It may be observed not only of Thomas Aquinas, but of the scholastic philosophers in general, that their double allegiance, to the Christian tradition and to Aristotle, resulted in a greater freedom than a single allegiance would have done. There was a close parallel to this in the political sphere, where in the Middle Ages individual liberty profited by the distinction and frequent rivalry between Church and State. In the strength of his citizenship, the individual could stand up against the one, in the strength of his churchmanship against the other, and in either case could depend on the support of a power universally respected, and able to defend those who relied upon it.

But if a double allegiance was favourable to individual freedom in the intellectual as in the political world, in both it was bound to lead to a collision between the two claimants to the allegiance of the same subject. The nations of modern Europe had received together the two great factors of their civilization, the tradition of classical antiquity, and that of the Christian Church. These were already combined when the barbarians entered into the inheritance of the Roman empire, which had then long professed Christianity. Rome, as at once the imperial city and the 'threshold of the apostles', where St. Peter and St. Paul were buried and their successor, the Pope, ruled in their name, was their link alike with the heroes of the one tradition and the sacred personages of the other. It was the work of the scholastic philosophy, in the new light shed on the former by the revelation, through a fresh channel, of a complete ancient philosophy, that of Aristotle, to make plain the deep-lying differences between the two traditions, and thereby to help in bringing about the dissolution of the medieval form of civilization which had rested upon a fusion of the two.

Very soon after the time of Abelard it became clear that a complete agreement such as he had hoped to see between philosophy and theology, in which the teachings of the former should altogether support and confirm those of the latter, was not to be looked for. Thomas Aquinas went a long way in an attempt to reconcile the two; but he was constrained to draw a sharp distinction between those theological doctrines which reason could find out for itself, and others for the discovery of which a supernatural revelation was necessary. It is worthy of remark that, in his work of reconciliation and of distinction, he was often treading (where the agreement of the Jewish and Christian religions permitted it) in the footsteps of a Jewish philosopher of the preceding century, Moses Maimonides (1135–1204). But other medieval thinkers found it a matter of greater difficulty to establish a satisfactory frontier between the dominions of the two rival powers: and some even went so far as to assert that there was a double standard of truth, that a thing might be true in philosophy, but not in theology, and vice versa. This doctrine, unsatisfactory as it is, probably served a useful purpose in securing for philosophers freedom to pursue their investigations in independence of theological tradition. On the other hand, if philosophy was not merely to exchange one yoke for another, it was desirable that it should not commit itself altogether to guides who ascribed to Aristotle the same infallibility which was claimed for the Bible and the Church. Hence it was of no small advantage to philosophy that on the problem of individual personality, to which the whole movement traced in our last chapter had given a greater prominence than it had enjoyed among the ancients, and which was of momentous interest to the theologian, Aristotle's teaching had been ambiguous and unsatisfactory.

We saw that the elementary logic books had long ago raised the question what was meant by a *genus* or a *species*. By the thirteenth century, a considerable measure of agreement had been reached as to the matter. Three kinds of 'universals'—natures, that is, common to several individuals and referred to when general terms are used—were usually recognized. In the first (or rather the last) place were the abstract general notions in our minds. I have, for example, seen many individual horses, and have a general notion of what they all have in common. But this general notion would be but a valueless figment if there were not, in the second place, something *really* common to all these individuals, not indeed separated from the accompanying differences, as it is in my notion of it, but yet really present *in* the individuals. Thirdly, it was not denied that in the mind of God there must have existed from all eternity the patterns of these common natures. Such 'universals existing before the individuals' Aristotle would not have admitted; but they were admitted, under the name of Ideas, on the express authority of Augustine, at a time when Aristotle was regarded as the teacher of logic only, and when his elaborate criticisms of Plato's theory of Ideas were not to hand. Now, however, the discussions in his *Metaphysics* of the nature of *substance*, that is, of what exists upon its own account and not merely as an attribute of something else, brought up the other side of the old question; for we certainly regard an individual man as a substance in this sense; and it was asked: 'What does one mean by an individual? How do individuals of the same species differ from one another?'

Upon this problem of the nature of individuality some of the best thought of the scholastic philosophers was expended. It is, in fact, a very difficult problem. For anything we state about an individual thing is at once a 'universal', which applies, or at any rate might apply, to other individuals beside this one. Might one not suppose two individuals exactly alike, so that whatever was said of one might as well be said of the other? Then what is it that makes them different individuals? If you say: Well, one is in this place and the other in that place, you can hardly have found where the real individuality of either lies: for many other things might be in either place, and these two may an instant hence have ceased to be where they now are.

Various views of this question were held by different Schoolmen, but the main tendency among them was in the direction of increasing the emphasis laid upon the importance of the individual. We see this in two philosophers who in many respects were poles apart in their views: Duns Scotus (who is said to have died in 1308), and William of Ockham (who died about 1350), both natives of the British Isles and both Franciscan friars. Duns was called in his day the 'subtle doctor', but a later generation, which despised his subtle arguments and highly valued the literary graces which he had neglected, came to use his name in the form 'dunce' to mean an illiterate dullard. What however now concerns us is his insistence that the individuality of e.g. a particular man is not to be looked upon as a limitation of the common nature of the human species, but rather as a higher perfection added to it.

William of Ockham went further. His rule not to multiply entities beyond what is necessary got the name of 'Ockham's razor', because it made a clean sweep of the subtle distinctions of which there was a luxuriant growth in the philosophy of other schoolmen, especially of Duns. Ockham applied this rule to the so-called 'universals', or common natures—such as *genera* and *species*. These, he held, have no existence beyond our minds, where they arise when we think of a number of similar individual things together and designate them by a common name. This doctrine is called Nominalism, or sometimes Conceptualism (because the *names* are, after all, no more than signs of our thoughts or *conceptions*). The opposite doctrine which attributes to universals or common natures a reality independent of our minds is called Realism. Now we have seen that the Christian religion, by the high value which is set on individual souls, had encouraged philosophy to concern itself more than it had done in antiquity with the problem of individual personality. But a thoroughgoing Nominalism, which denied that several real beings could really be one, though they might be considered by a single act of the mind or called by a single name, was difficult—except by the help of the strange doctrine, already mentioned, of a double truth—to reconcile with certain Christian doctrines, and especially with that of the Trinity. Thus Nominalism was a view in putting forward which Ockham and his followers gave expression to a general desire to escape from the trammels of tradition, whether classical or Christian; while at the same time, revolutionary movement as it was, it was still true to that concentration of interest on individual personality which, on the whole, had distinguished the thought of the Christian era from that of classical antiquity.

CHAPTER VI

PHILOSOPHY AT THE COMING OF AGE OF MODERN EUROPE

IN the title of our last chapter, the Middle Ages were called the 'minority' of modern Europe; in the title of this, the name of its 'coming of age' is given to what is commonly known as the Renaissance, the new birth, that is, of literature and art under the inspiration of a greatly increased knowledge of the literature and art of classical antiquity, which took place in the fourteenth, fifteenth, and sixteenth centuries. A brief history of philosophy like this can only afford to touch very lightly on many aspects of this great movement, which yet influenced philosophers no less than other men.

Politically, the great peoples of modern Europe, the English, the French, the Spaniards, the Germans, the Italians, had arrived at a stage of their development where they were too keenly conscious that they were separate nations, each with a common life, common interests, common ambitions of its own, not to be impatient of the restraints imposed upon these by the international institutions of the Middle Ages, under whose tutelage they had grown up to maturity. Such institutions were the Catholic Church, under its earthly head, the Pope of Rome; the Empire, which claimed to be that very Roman empire into which the barbarian ancestors of the modern nations had pressed long ago, and whose civilization and religion they had adopted; and the feudal system, which bound men to one another in an intricate network of ties of lordship and vassalage, which might, and not infrequently did, cut right across the lines of demarcation between nations. Of these three, the Empire was by this time the least important; for its international pretensions had become little more than a claim to ceremonial precedence over other sovereigns on the part of the German kings, who had long enjoyed the imperial dignity practically as a matter of course. Yet, in the two countries which were considered to be immediately subject to it, Germany and Italy, this claim, by putting every one who owned no superior but the emperor on a level with sovereigns elsewhere, retarded the rise of a single national sovereignty, and so prevented until the nineteenth century the attainment of such a national unity as England, France, and Spain had long enjoyed.

At the period we have now reached, however, the nations had grown impatient of international restraints; and among individuals too a spirit was spreading, to which the intellectual authority of Aristotle and the religious authority of the Church were apt to appear no longer in the guise of welcome guides, but rather of encroaching tyrannies. This spirit eventually combined with the impulse to national self-assertion to produce the religious movement usually called the Reformation, in the course of which the repudiation of the papal supremacy in England, Scotland, Holland, Scandinavia, and parts of Germany and Switzerland, broke up the ecclesiastical unity of Europe.

Philosophy profited by this great movement of disruption, not so much because the separated Churches taught doctrines which invited philosophical criticism less than those of the body from which they had separated, nor because their teachers and rulers were always less tolerant of such criticism than the Catholic priesthood, but because an authority deriving its origin from a recent revolution has inevitably less power of offering effectual resistance to further change than one which has been so long acknowledged, that the memory of man runs not to the contrary. Of the movement itself the chief leader was the German, Martin Luther (1483–1546). The famous doctrine which was the foundation of his teaching, that a man is justified by faith alone, not by works, has a double aspect. On the one hand, it aims at making the individual independent in his religious life of any system of ordinances and penances which the Church may prescribe. He has only whole-heartedly to trust in the promises of God. On the other hand, the same faith, according to Luther, dispenses the individual from the anxious scrutiny of his own inner condition and spiritual attainment, so much encouraged in the monastic life of celibacy and retirement from the world, which to the men of the Middle Ages had seemed the most truly Christian life, but which Luther himself had, after personal experience of it, ceased to regard in this light. So dispensed, the ordinary duties of a householder and citizen lie open to him as the natural sphere of human activity, in which he need not scruple to take part.

The principle of the Reformation, regarded in this light, is in close agreement with the general attitude of the age in which it was put forward. It was an age in which the individual was asserting his independence, not, however, for the most part, as in earlier times, in order to turn his eyes inward, and occupy himself with the secrets of his own heart, but rather to be free to look about him, and enjoy the feast of good things which God and nature had spread before him. For there was opening before modern Europe at this its coming of age a world of wider horizons and richer in the materials of enjoyment than its childhood had known. To adventure oneself upon it by taking one's share of its work and its chances of good and evil seemed the call of duty; to turn one's back upon it and take refuge in a cloister cowardly and ungrateful.

The widening of horizons and increase of the materials of enjoyment had come, in the first place, through the revival in the west of the study of Greek, which could now be learned from Greek scholars whom the advancing arms of the Turks (who in 1453 captured Constantinople) had driven to take refuge in Italy. This opened up treasures both of knowledge and of poetry hitherto closed against the learned of the west. They could read in the original what they had so far only read in translations; they could read much that they had hitherto not read at all. For example, acquaintance could now be made at first hand with the philosophy of Plato; and Aristotle himself could be read in his own tongue and apart from the glosses of medieval schoolmen, whether Arabian or Latin. Moreover, the keen interest excited in all that related to classical literature did not limit itself to Greek books. Those works of ancient Latin authors which were already read were studied afresh with the help of a better knowledge of their time; and others long forgotten were brought again to light. To the new sense of nationality the political thought of the ancient Greeks and Romans was more congenial than medieval theories of a united Christendom under Pope and

Emperor. For, although the city-states of classical antiquity were not national states, they were at any rate separate and independent commonwealths, each with the defence of its interests against hostile neighbours for its most sacred trust. The ideal of an independent national state inspired the *Prince* of Niccolò Machiavelli (1469–1527), who wished to see such an one established in his native Italy; it inspired also, more than a century later, the *Leviathan* of Thomas Hobbes (1588–1679), who during the English civil war expounded the principles on which he held all such states to be based, for a generation which seemed to him, for lack of understanding these principles, to be ready under one pretext or another to impair the unity and efficiency of the sovereign power, which both writers (here differing from most of the ancients) regard as normally, though not necessarily, concentrated in the hand of a single absolute ruler.

But it was not only classical antiquity which was no longer to be seen through a mist of medieval tradition; a clearer view could also be obtained of primitive Christianity. In consequence, men were more easily induced to challenge the right of existing ecclesiastical institutions to claim the authority of an age in which it was generally admitted that the Christian religion, being nearest its fountainhead, must have been at its purest.

Moreover, of space as well as of time a vaster range was open to the survey of the men of the Renaissance than that with which their fathers had had to do. In 1492 the voyage of Columbus had revealed to Europe a new inhabited world beyond the ocean. The great epoch of discovery which thus began immensely stimulated the thirst for new knowledge, and raised men's hopes of obtaining it. The pillars of Hercules, as the ancients had called them—the straits of Gibraltar, as we say—could no longer be looked upon as bounds set by nature in that direction to the enterprise of the dwellers in Europe. The device of a ship in full sail setting out between those pillars to explore the western seas was chosen by Francis Bacon (1561–1626), the chief representative of English philosophy during the period which we are describing, to adorn the frontispiece of his *Instauratio Magna*, or *Grand Renovation of Philosophy*. In the work planned under this ambitious title, of which he only wrote a small part, and which, indeed, he did not hope to complete, the author aimed at nothing less than the construction of a new philosophy based on a survey, carried out by a new method, of all the principal kinds of natural phenomena.

For, of all the means by which the men of the Renaissance succeeded in passing the limits within which medieval knowledge of the universe had been confined, that which carried them and was destined to carry their successors by far the furthest was their closer attention to natural phenomena. This closer attention is a feature of the last rather than of the earlier stages of the movement; it is especially characteristic of the sixteenth century. Natural science had throughout the Middle Ages been neglected in comparison with logic, metaphysics, and theology. Men like the English Franciscan friar, Roger Bacon, in the thirteenth century, who made the investigation of nature his chief business and urged its claims to greater consideration, were apt to be suspected of heterodoxy. Among the common folk such men were often regarded as wizards in league with evil spirits. Not only was this the case with Roger Bacon himself, but even the Dominican Albertus Magnus, the master of Thomas Aquinas, and honoured by the Church as 'the blessed Albert', figures as a conjurer in popular legend on account of his reputation for natural knowledge. The fact that experimental science was represented by the alchemists, who aimed at discovering a way of transmuting the baser metals into gold and affected much secrecy in their operations, tended to encourage an association in men's minds between the knowledge of natural processes and the pursuit of worldly objects by mysterious means.

Francis Bacon's design was, by means of inquiries some of which should be experimental like those of the alchemists, but purged from all superstitious taint and directed not toward immediate gain, but toward a thoroughgoing knowledge, vastly to increase in the long run the dominion of man over nature. To enjoy such a dominion was, he held, the original destiny of our race. But in a vain and impious attempt (described in the Biblical story as 'eating of the tree of knowledge of good and evil') to make laws for himself by 'moral philosophy', instead of remaining content with the positive commands of God, man had turned aside from his proper business of pursuing 'natural philosophy', that is, of studying and interpreting the works of God and raising in his own intelligence a true image of the universe; gaining, in other words, such a knowledge of nature's inner workings as may make it possible to emulate them. The failure of men hitherto to do this, and the depressing tradition that the processes of chemical combination were necessarily

beyond the reach of human imitation, showed only
that ancient theories of nature were merely superficial
and had not penetrated her true secrets. But 'in
the sweat of his brow' man may yet 'eat his bread',
that is, through resolute and patient persistence in
discriminating observation and well-devised experiment, he may wring these secrets from her and turn
them to his own advantage. For this, however, a new
method of approach is necessary; and this Bacon
endeavoured to provide in his *Novum Organum*, that is
'the New Instrument', which was to take the place of
the old *Organon*, namely the collection of Aristotle's
treatises on logic, which were so called as constituting
the proper 'instrument' to be used in reasoning,
whatever one was reasoning about.

Nature, Bacon urged, is too complex for so simple a
method as the syllogism, which the scholastic tradition
maintained by the custom of disputation as the means
of qualifying for University degrees, regarded as the
only scientific method, to be 'adequate to its subtlety'.
A syllogism, moreover, could only draw conclusions
from admitted premises. In practice, the premises
admitted were hasty generalizations from superficial
experience or statements made by Aristotle or other
authorities, which, in deference to a supposed axiom
that no science could question its own first principles,
were not submitted to re-examination. The supposed
axiom in question was a perversion of a maxim of
Aristotle, originally intended to express the truth that
every principal science has a subject-matter of its
own (as e.g. arithmetic has numbers, geometry has
figures in space) to which our reasonings within that
science, if they are not to lose themselves in vague

generalities, must be careful to confine themselves. By his insistence upon this truth Aristotle had rendered an important service to science; but his maxim had, in Bacon's judgement, come to be used to check the free play of criticism on established beliefs about nature, which (though often very questionable) were allowed so to prejudice the minds of students that to facts which did not support them no attention was paid. Bacon would have the inquirer attend to all facts. He was to 'enter the kingdom of nature, like the kingdom of grace, as a little child', to learn, and not to dictate. Nature could only be conquered by obeying her. Nor could she be conquered by isolated efforts. Such discoveries as had been made had frequently been lost again through lack of a provision for recording them. Not until there was a systematic collection and preservation of facts (which could not be without greater expense than private fortunes could support) would it be reasonable to look for a properly based philosophy of nature.

In these observations, Bacon showed a true insight into the needs and prospects of natural science; and his eloquent announcement of them was found inspiring in the next generation by Robert Boyle, the 'father of chemistry', and the other founders of the Royal Society. But neither they nor any other men of science followed in detail the method proposed by Bacon. He called this method a 'true Induction'. It had been usual to contrast Induction with Syllogism, in the sense of a process by which a number of particular instances (all, if possible) were brought forward to establish or confirm a general rule; while Syllogism would show it to follow from the combination of yet more general

principles. Bacon, wishing to set up, by the side of
Syllogism, a method better suited to the requirements
of natural science, called this Induction, as starting
from facts, not from assumptions; unlike, however,
Induction in the older sense, it was to take even more
account of 'negative instances' than of positive—that
is (to use the phraseology of John Stuart Mill, who in
1843 attempted in his *System of Logic* to remodel the
Baconian method in the light of the actual progress
of the sciences) of cases 'in which the phenomenon
under investigation is absent', than of cases in which
it is present.

Natural science can only be said to employ Bacon's
inductive method in the very general sense that it
agrees with it in starting from facts, in noting negative
instances, and in employing systematically collected
records of past experience; not in the sense that it
uses the special method laid down in the *Novum
Organum*. Bacon, then, did not, as he hoped to do,
supply investigators of nature with an infallible
method; he underrated the immensity of the task
before them; he himself made no contribution of
first-rate importance to the stock of natural knowledge;
to those questions about the nature of ultimate reality
which we have regarded as the distinctive interest of
philosophy he was not specially attracted. But he
devoted a magnificent style and extraordinary powers
of mind to the mission of proclaiming the glorious
destinies of natural science and the truth (which the
Middle Ages had practically ignored) that without a
genuine and progressive study of natural phenomena
philosophy will be, at the least, half starved. His own
description of himself as *buccinator novi temporis*, the

trumpeter of a new age, describes, perhaps as well as it could be described, his real position in the history of thought.

The age of Bacon was one of great progress in the natural sciences; but their most eloquent champion showed himself by no means especially ready to welcome the chief results of this progress. Of his countryman, William Gilbert (1540–1603), the founder of the sciences of electricity and magnetism, he speaks more often with censure than with approbation; and he ignored the great discovery of the true nature of the circulation of the blood made by his own physician, William Harvey (1578–1657), who, indeed, said of him, in contempt of his scientific pretensions, that he wrote philosophy like (what he was at the time) a Lord Chancellor. Nor did he bring himself to accept the theory, the triumph of which has, more than anything else, made the medieval view of the universe seem remote and strange to us. This was the theory put forward by the Polish mathematician Nicolaus Copernicus in 1543, and confirmed by the discoveries made with the lately invented telescope, in Bacon's own time and within his knowledge, by the Italian Galileo Galilei (1564–1642), whose account of scientific method is now very commonly acknowledged to be superior to Bacon's, especially in its recognition of the part which hypothesis and mathematical reasoning must play in the development of natural science. It was the theory that the earth rotates daily upon its axis, and that the sun, and not the earth, is the centre about which the planets (and the earth among them) revolve.

Although this theory was not unknown in classical

antiquity, it never succeeded (in the absence of the confirmation given by the telescope) in winning the general assent of astronomers, and in the Middle Ages it was not likely to be revived in view of the fact that the rival hypothesis, according to which the earth is motionless and the heavens revolve about it, had on its side not only the apparent evidence of the senses and the language of the Bible, but also the authority both of Aristotle and of the man whose book, known as the *Almagest*, was the chief source of astronomical knowledge for the scholars of the time, the astronomer Ptolemy, who lived in the second century of our era.

The Copernican theory, which Bacon rejected, a contemporary of his, Giordano Bruno (1548–1600), enthusiastically welcomed. He rejoiced in the freedom of an infinite universe which it seemed to open up. The old distinction which both popular religion and the Aristotelian philosophy had drawn between 'the heavens' and 'the earth' had vanished with the belief that the latter was fixed and the former in motion. The earth could now be regarded as all of one piece with the heavens, and no less divine than they.

The new theory was not allowed to pass unchallenged by those who feared the effect of such a revolution in the view of the physical relations between man and his dwelling-place upon the sentiments of men toward a religion the language of whose sacred books and formularies everywhere implied the older way of looking at the matter. Bruno was tried for the venturesome speculations to which his acceptance of the new theory had led, and burned alive by the sentence of the Inquisition at Rome in 1600; and in 1633 the same tribunal forced the aged Galileo to retract as heretical the doctrine of the earth's motion. A legend, for it is no more, told that, as the great astronomer rose from his knees after recanting, he said 'All the same, it moves!' The story is, no doubt, true to the inner thought of him of whom it is told; and it expresses what after generations feel when they read of the recantation. The persecutions of the Inquisition were of no avail against the progress of the truth the proclamation of which they attempted to check. They may have made some thinkers more cautious in their phraseology; but, from this time onwards, there has been no philosopher who has seriously doubted the daily revolution of the earth upon its own axis, or its annual revolution about the sun. The old belief in a fixed earth set in the centre of a limited number of revolving spheres was dead for ever.

CHAPTER VII

DESCARTES AND HIS SUCCESSORS

WE have reached in our history an age in which, for educated men, the stage of 'heaven and earth', on which for so many centuries the drama of human life had been played, had been suddenly discovered to be, as it were, a mere illusion of the theatre, which would vanish if the spectator did but shift his seat. The earth which, it had been thought, was 'made so fast that it could not be moved', was found to be in fact for ever on the move; while the Sun, so far as his daily course was concerned, of which poets had delighted from time immemorial to sing as coming forth from his chamber to run from one end of the heaven to the other, was all the while standing still. No wonder if, in such an age, the inquisitive mind of the Frenchman René Descartes (1596–1650) should have felt any conviction which he had yet entertained to be insecure until tested by the touchstone of a deliberate attempt to doubt it.

Accordingly in 1619 he undertook to carry doubt as far as it would go; and the upshot was that he found one thing which he could not doubt, namely his own existence. For even to doubt he must think, and to think he must exist. Hence the bedrock of certainty is this: *Cogito, ergo sum*; I think, therefore I am. We must bear in mind that what he finds thus indubitable is only his existence as a thinking being, not as the individual with this particular body, born on a particular day, and so forth. Descartes would not say 'As sure as that I stand here', but only 'as sure as that I am now thinking'. I might be under a delusion as to the position of my body, nay, as to my having a body at all; but not as to my thinking, in the broad sense in which Descartes uses the word to include any kind of mental operation of which I may be conscious. I can, however, go further. This consciousness of myself, which does not admit of doubt, I shall find on examining it to be a consciousness of self as something imperfect, limited, finite, and therefore as involving an idea of something perfect and infinite, with which I contrast myself and find myself fall short of it. Here we meet with the word 'idea' in the sense with which we are nowadays most familiar.

How did it come to bear such a meaning, so different from that which we saw it bore in Plato's philosophy? The explanation is, briefly, that the eternal natures, the objects of knowledge strictly so called, to which Plato gave the name, came by later thinkers and especially by Augustine, who would not admit anything to be eternal beside God, to be regarded as God's eternal thoughts, related to the objects of our experience as the designs in an artist's mind to the works of his hands. From meaning 'thoughts in the divine mind', the word was extended in the sixteenth century, when the general revolt against the tyranny of Aristotle favoured a word which he had discarded, to thoughts in the human mind also, and began to take a place in the vocabulary of philosophy which had in the Middle Ages been filled by *species*, not in the sense of a 'kind' in which we know it best, but in that of something intermediate between our minds and the independently existing things of which they are aware, and representing within the mind what exists on its own account outside of it.

It is in such a sense that 'idea' was used both by Descartes and by his English contemporary and correspondent Hobbes. Hobbes, however, would not agree with Descartes that we could be said to have the idea of an infinitely perfect being. This was because Hobbes always meant by an idea something which was the result of an impression on the organs of sense. Hobbes was not disinclined to conjecture the existence of an eternal power, the cause of all that happens in the world, which one may call God; but of this power, as distinct from its effects, which alone affect our senses, and so give rise to ideas, we can, he held, form no definite conception or idea. Descartes thought otherwise. There are other things, he pointed out, of which we can have an idea in the sense of a definite conception, which yet we cannot picture to ourselves with the same definiteness, such as, for example, a figure with a thousand sides. Of a perfect being we have a positive and in that sense definite, though not a detailed, conception. Yet this 'idea' cannot be supposed to be derived from ourselves whom we perceive to be imperfect, and just in that very perception become aware of the perfection of which we fall short. Its presence, then, within us is inexplicable except on the supposition of a real being which is its original. And indeed (so Descartes argues) the idea of a perfect being implies, as no other does, the real existence of such a being. For, while with any other being of which I may have an idea there is no contradiction involved in thinking of it as something which might exist, but actually does not, the notion

of an absolutely perfect being which does not exist
is as self-contradictory as that of a hill without a valley,
or of a triangle whose angles are not equal to two right
angles. It would be the notion of a perfect being
which, as lacking reality, was imperfect.

This argument is usually known as the Ontological
Argument for the existence of God. Although it is
called an argument for the existence of God, we must
not think of it as proving by itself the existence of a
being such as we generally mean by the word 'God';
a being with whom it is possible to establish what we
may call personal relations of worship and com-
munion. What it does is something different from
this. In the first place, it points out the consciousness
of an infinite or perfect nature implied in our consciousness of our own finitude or imperfection; in the
second, it gives a striking expression to a conviction
which only the most extreme scepticism can even
pretend altogether to have laid aside, namely the conviction that all thought and consciousness is thought
and consciousness of something real. When we make
mistakes (as we often do), we are not conscious of
anything real, but only of mistaking one real thing for
another, or of thinking of two real things as together
which are really apart, or of two real things as apart
which are really together.

The cause of such mistaking, Descartes thought, was
always some degree of wilfulness, if only that of
judging one way or the other when one did not really
know. Moreover, unless we possessed a capacity of
distinguishing genuine knowledge from what is not
such, we should not be able to avoid making such
mistakes, or to correct them when made. Such a

capacity, however, Descartes held that we did possess. When our perceptions are *clear* and *distinct*, when there is no obscurity in what we perceive, and we are aware too that, besides what is thus plain to us, there is nothing else present in what we perceive, then the only doubt that can remain is the doubt whether we may not be the dupes of some malignant demon which finds pleasure in deceiving us. This doubt is removed when we are convinced of the existence of God, the perfect being, the idea of which we could not have unless such an one there were; for among God's perfections veracity must be included, and by the divine veracity what is clear and distinct to us by the light of nature is guaranteed. We will not look for flaws in this argument, but content ourselves with noting that in this way the warrant of such clear and distinct knowledge as is yielded by the mathematical sciences, of which Descartes was a great master, is found in the perfection of God, and that this in its turn is considered to be involved in that knowledge of one's own existence as a thinking being which we may gain even from the act of doubting whatever can be doubted.

In thus taking the mind which thinks as the one indubitable fact which can serve as a starting point, and leaving it as a question to be subsequently determined whether there exists anything else outside of it corresponding to its 'ideas', which are described as if they were known at first only as part of it, the philosophy of Descartes (and much other modern philosophy with it) stands in sharp contrast with that of antiquity. The Greek philosophers may be said, speaking generally, to have taken as beyond doubt the existence of a real world, including the mind, which fulfils its peculiar function in apprehending the rest. No doubt, they held that much seemed real that was not; but that something was real they considered as beyond question. Medieval philosophy, although, under the influence of Christianity, it might exalt the human spirit to the highest place among created things, and even regard (in this departing from its master, Aristotle) the physical universe as existing for its sake, did not break away from the conviction which it inherited from antiquity that the existence of something real other than the human mind was beyond question. Descartes did thus break away in doubting the existence of everything but his own mind. Nor could he recover himself from this doubt except by the help of the Ontological Argument which, in assuring him of the existence of God from the consideration that his own nature as a thinking being implies it, guaranteed also the existence of a world corresponding to his clear and distinct ideas. Without this argument he would have been left with no certainty that anything existed beyond the thinking mind.

Now this argument had been brought forward already by one of the earliest and greatest of medieval thinkers, Anselm, who was Archbishop of Canterbury from 1093 till his death in 1109. But the Schoolmen, not having parted company from the ancients' unquestioning certainty that a real world beyond the mind existed, did not appreciate its importance; and it never attracted so much attention in the Middle Ages as it has in modern times since its revival by Descartes.

Our clear and distinct knowledge being thus guaranteed, it is important to observe what knowledge is to be considered as having this character. We have seen already that mathematical knowledge has it; and, for Descartes, only such knowledge of bodies is 'clear and distinct' as is either mathematical and relates to them considered as extended in space, or mechanical and relates to them as moving in space from one point to another. Extension is the essence of body; for whatever other attributes a body may have besides, it may cease to have without ceasing to be a body. That which fills space is capable of being divided *ad infinitum*, and of being variously shaped or figured; the infinitely numerous parts may be variously joined or disjoined, thus producing the various figures; and such rearrangement is possible only through motion. Nothing about bodies, then, but their occupancy of space, their shape, and their motion can be clearly and distinctly conceived. In all other attributes which we commonly ascribe to bodies, such as colour or warmth or sound, there is mixed something which does not belong to the bodies themselves, but to our souls which perceive them; and if we take these attributes as we find them, and try to conceive of them as belonging to the bodies we call coloured or warm or whatever it may be, we shall find ourselves beset with all sorts of puzzles and as far as possible from 'clear and distinct' knowledge.

This refusal to consider any attributes of bodies as really belonging to them apart from our perception of them which are not susceptible of mathematical and mechanical treatment was also made in antiquity by Democritus and, among Descartes' own contemporaries, by Galileo and by Hobbes. The importance of it is that it clears the way for a consistently mechanical treatment of the physical universe. An attempt at such a treatment could at this period be made under more satisfactory conditions than had ever before obtained, owing to the establishment by Kepler (1571–1630), Galileo, and Descartes himself of what were afterwards, as formulated by Sir Isaac Newton, called the first and second laws of motion. The former of these is the law that a body must continue in a state of rest or of uniform motion in a straight line unless acted on by some external force. The latter is the law that change of motion (which must thus be due to a new force acting upon the body, beside that which first set it in motion) takes place in the direction of the newly impressed force, and is proportional to it; the resulting motion thus being a composition of the original motion with that which the second force would have impressed had the body been at rest when it began to act upon it.

In their interest in the attempt to explain the phenomena of physical nature on mathematical and mechanical principles alone, Hobbes and Descartes were at one; but Hobbes went further. He thought it possible to see not only in all physical processes, but also in consciousness, a kind of motion. To Descartes, on the other hand, it seemed meaningless to speak either of a mind or consciousness as in motion, or of a body as thinking or conscious. We have, he held, a clear and distinct idea of extension apart from thinking, and of thinking apart from extension. For this reason, he could call that which was extended, or matter, and that which was conscious, or mind, alike by the name of 'substances', that is, things existing on their own account; because each could be conceived

—indeed, could only be conceived—as independent of the other. But this sharp contrast of mind and matter, as two things quite independent of one another, presents an obvious difficulty when we think of their intimate union in our own persons. The problem of this union gave Descartes and his followers no little trouble. Organic bodies of all kinds they regarded as machines; whatever happened within them was to be explained on the mechanical principles which, as we have seen, were applied to the physical universe of which they form part. States of mind, on the other hand, seemed as little capable of being explained by bodily movements as bodily movements by states of mind. Yet, assuredly, in our own experience bodily movements and states of mind appear to affect one another. The attempts of Descartes himself to get over this difficulty were far from successful. It gave away the case for the impossibility of interaction between soul and body, without making it in the least more intelligible, to say that it took place only at one point in the body, in what is called the pineal gland in the brain, and only there through what Descartes described as the 'animal spirits'. These he supposed to be a subtle kind of fluid, distilled in the heart from the finest particles of the blood and driven, on strictly mechanical principles, from the heart to the brain, and thence through the nerves and muscles. The motions of these spirits were the cause of all the spontaneous movements of animals, but were in human beings capable of being directed, although not originated, by the soul. These 'animal spirits' were a mere figment; and, though there is really such a thing in the human body as the pineal gland, there is no good reason for supposing it to be the seat of the soul; and, even if it were otherwise, the difficulty they were invoked to solve remains just where it was before.

More consistent was the theory known as Occasionalism, which afterwards obtained among the Cartesians (as the followers of Descartes are called), and is especially associated with the name of Arnold Geulincx (1625–69). According to this view, there is really no interaction between body and soul: the appearance of it must be referred to the action of God, an absolute dependence upon whom is the only thing which they have in common. The stimulation of my optic nerve by the sun's rays is not the cause of my sensation of light; but on *occasion* of the former, God causes in me the latter. Nor is my will to move my hand the cause of its movement; but on *occasion* of the former, God causes the latter to take place. We need not, however, think of the occasion in the second instance as arising independently of God, any more than in the first, where it is the result of the universal laws of matter and motion which his will has established. He is the cause of our willing as well as of our bodily movements; and so the relation of body and soul may be compared to that between two clocks wound up to keep time together, so that to every movement of the one will exactly correspond a movement of the other. Occasionalism thus supposes the mind or soul, when it is what we call 'perceiving', to depend immediately upon God, without any mediation of the bodies which it is commonly said to perceive; while, on the other hand, it holds that only through the mediation of God can souls and bodies come together.

Another Cartesian, the Oratorian priest Nicolas

Malebranche (1638–1715), only carried these views a little further when he taught that the clear and distinct idea of extension or body which we have when we apprehend its mathematical qualities—since, being an *idea*, it cannot belong to the extended world of bodies, nor, being an idea of *extension*, to the mind, to which extension is on the principles of Descartes utterly foreign—can only belong to God, in whom alone the two kinds of being come together. Hence, according to Malebranche, what we really have before us in apprehending bodies as the mathematician does are not ideas of our own minds, but ideas of God, the eternal patterns of the bodies which make up the extended or material world; we thus may be said to 'see all things in God'. We may note that this theory explains 'ideas' in Descartes' sense of 'human thoughts' as 'ideas' in Augustine's sense of divine thoughts; and Augustine was a thinker for whom Malebranche had an especial admiration.

The philosophy of Descartes and his followers sets matter and mind, extension and thought, over against one another, each being just what the other is not, and having nothing in common with the other but a continual dependence upon the source of all existence, God. This dependence, however, would justify a strict Cartesian in refusing to either of them the title of a 'substance', if by 'substance' we mean what Descartes meant, something which can be conceived as completely independent of anything else. This refusal was actually made by a thinker who began his philosophical career as a Cartesian, but is too great a man to be reckoned merely among the followers of any one else, the Jew Baruch, or Benedict, Spinoza (1632–77).

For him, there was but one Substance, God or Nature, of which extension and thought are to be regarded as 'attributes'. We have, he holds, no reason for supposing them to be the only attributes of this substance; but to us no others are known. As with the Occasionalists, so with Spinoza, these two 'attributes' never interact with one another or overlap one another. The nature of God or the universe may be expressed in terms of either. There is what may be called a complete parallelism between them, so that there can be nothing in the mind which is not the 'idea' or mental counterpart of something bodily or material; nor anything in the material world of which there is not a corresponding 'idea'.

To the whole material system corresponds such an understanding of it as is the goal of the physicist, an understanding in which there is no thought of purposes or 'final causes', but only of a mathematical or mechanical necessity. Such an imperfect apprehension of it as any one of us actually has—and which constitutes his 'soul'—is primarily a consciousness of that part of the system which is called his 'body', and of any other parts only so far as they are in direct or indirect contact with this. All in our 'souls' that has reference to our 'bodies' as things taken apart from the whole system of material nature (or, as Spinoza would say, of God under the attribute of extension) only belongs to them so far as they themselves are similarly taken out of their context in the complete system of thought which he calls 'the infinite understanding of God'. Such are the emotions which correspond to the effort by which a particular body maintains for a while its separate existence. Such again is the sense of acting spontaneously and for purposes of our own, which we experience when our movements are immediately due to processes within our bodies, the more remote causes of which lie in a region of the material universe which is beyond our ken. Thus what is sometimes called our consciousness of the freedom of our wills turns out to be in Spinoza's judgement merely a result of the combination of direct perception of the effect with ignorance of the cause. If a stone, after being thrown into the air, should by some miracle become conscious, it would find itself moving, yet be ignorant of what set it in motion, and might naturally suppose its movements due solely to itself. We are, in respect of what we suppose to be our spontaneous acts, in the position of such a stone.

It may, indeed, be doubted whether the consciousness of freedom which we have in certain cases can be thus explained away, and whether, if placed in the position of the stone in Spinoza's illustration, we should suppose ourselves to be acting freely. But, however that may be, we must observe that Spinoza does not hold that, in discovering this supposed consciousness of freedom to be due merely to the imperfection of our knowledge, we need feel ourselves robbed of anything truly valuable. There is, he thinks, a much more precious kind of consciousness of freedom which comes not from ignorance, but from knowledge. In proportion as a man sees in all that he is and does and suffers, a consequence of the eternal and unchangeable nature of the universe, or, as Spinoza would say, of God, he is delivered from the bondage in which he remains, at the mercy of vain hopes and fears, so long as he thinks of himself as having interests and possibilities of his own apart from the whole of which he forms a part. Spinoza can take this view because he is sure that no satisfaction and peace can be greater than those which come in the train of knowledge, and which culminate in what he calls 'the intellectual love of God'. He does not mean by this expression a sentiment such as we may entertain towards another person who loves us, or who we hope may love us in return. In this love of God, there is no more question of reciprocation than in that of which Aristotle had spoken. Alike to Aristotle and to Spinoza, God's own knowledge and enjoyment can only be a knowledge and enjoyment of his own nature.

But here the resemblance between the two philosophers ends. For Aristotle nowhere speaks as though our being were included within God's, or our knowledge and love of God within God's knowledge and love of himself. Spinoza, on the other hand, teaches that our understanding or knowledge of God is a part of God's infinite understanding or knowledge of himself, and our 'intellectual love' of him a part of the infinite love with which God loves himself. We may even speak of a love of God for us; but this is not a different thing from our love for God. The love of God for himself, of which our love for God is part, is a love for ourselves, because our minds and the thoughts which constitute them, so far as they think clearly and thoroughly, are parts of that one eternal system of thought which is God viewed under the 'attribute of thought', just as our bodies are parts of that eternal system of matter in motion which is God viewed under the 'attribute of extension'. Though Spinoza spoke so much of God, he seemed to mean by the word something so different from what was meant by it in the language of most religious teachers that, for a long time, he was commonly regarded as an atheist and the very chief of atheists. But, if by an atheist be meant a man without religion, no name could be less suitably applied to Spinoza, who found the most exalted language of religion no more than adequate to describe the impression made upon him by the contemplation of that nature which was revealed alike in the laws of matter and motion, and in the laws of the thought which can discover these.

In this contemplation, however, it is not easy to see what individuality is left to particular human minds. Just as your body or mine, regarded purely from the point of view of the physicist, is all of one piece with the whole world of matter and motion, and no more marked off from the rest than any larger or smaller portion of that world that it might happen to be convenient to select for consideration, so also in your thought or mine, so far as it attains to a strictly scientific understanding of the laws of this world of matter and motion, and of the thinker's body in its true relation to the whole, there does not seem to be anything special to you or to me, unless it be that to each of us a different bit of that world, namely his own body, must be as it were in the foreground. Now we must observe that in Spinoza's age, which was the age of Galileo and of Newton (who was born in 1642, the year of Galileo's death), it was on the problems of mechanics and physics that the attention of scientific students of nature was concentrated; and it is just in reference to these that individuality, whether of body or soul, seems to be of least account. The biologist cannot treat as indifferent the question what entitles a particular organism, a plant or an animal, to be considered an individual of its kind; but the physicist is not concerned with the distinction between organisms and other bodies, only with the laws of motion and gravity, to which all bodies, organic or inorganic, are equally subject. So, too, although no doubt differences between individual minds are sufficiently apparent in the capacity to discover and to grasp the truths of mathematics and mechanics, yet the truths themselves are so abstract that when they are once discovered and grasped the work of the individual discoverers seems to be done. These results become common property: and the ordinary student of them does not need to seek them in the works of their first discoverers, which thus come to have a purely historical interest. It is not so with the work of poets and of artists, of moral and religious teachers, or of philosophers in the sense in which we are using the word in this book. The substance of what these say cannot be so separated from the personality which their utterances express and stated anew as to make it unnecessary to seek it in the works of those who said it first.

This is true among others of Spinoza himself; but his ideal of knowledge is so much that of the mathematician and physicist that it is no wonder it should have caused the contemporary best capable of understanding his philosophy to set himself so to correct its chief defect as to do justice to that plurality of individuals which seemed in Spinoza's system to be in danger of losing their distinct individualities in the unity of the one Substance. This was the German Gottfried Wilhelm Leibniz (1646–1716), who thus takes up again that question of the principle of individuality to which the Schoolmen had devoted so much of their attention. Although Descartes had found the bedrock of certainty in the thinker's indubitable conviction of his own existence, his interests, like Spinoza's, were so concentrated on mathematical and mechanical problems that, while he emphasized to the full the difference between thought and extension, mind and matter, he did not dwell on the difference between one individual thinker and another; and what he says of his own existence might as well be said of *any* individual thinker's.

A greater contrast than that which existed between the personal character and circumstances of Spinoza and those of Leibniz can scarcely be imagined. After his excommunication for heresy at the age of twenty-four by the authorities of the Jewish synagogue at Amsterdam, Spinoza remained in Holland, living a life of the greatest simplicity, untrammelled by domestic ties or official duties, supporting himself by the grinding of lenses, and refusing any offer of emolument by the acceptance of which he might compromise his independence. Thus he could devote himself wholeheartedly to his scientific and philosophical studies, without need either to conceal his opinions or to engage in controversy. Leibniz, on the other hand, was a courtier and a man of affairs, with whom science and philosophy only formed a part, though no doubt the chief part, of his activities. He busied himself also with the founding of learned societies, with attempts to reconcile the Catholic and Protestant Churches, with the history of the princely house of Hanover, in whose employment he was, with the collection of treaties and other documents of international importance. His wide knowledge of the history of opinions led him to the view that schools and sects were most often right in their affirmations and wrong in their denials, and so to desire to insist, where he could, on points of agreement between his own theories and those of others. In this there was nothing unworthy; but it laid him open to the temptation of slurring over the points of disagreement; and he has been reproached with a cowardly reticence concerning the extent of his obligations as a philosopher to Spinoza, who enjoyed an evil reputation among the majority of his contemporaries as an enemy of religion.

It was thus the nature of individuality to which Leibniz turned his attention. Where was true individuality to be found? Not in the physical atom, though the word 'atom' means in Greek what 'individual' means in Latin. For, although there might be particles of matter which could not be actually divided, yet they must be extended in space and so have parts, even if no force exists capable of separating these parts from one another. Nay, these parts must be themselves divisible, and so on *ad infinitum*; and one cannot hope to come to real individuality, real indivisible unity, however far one goes. The unity, therefore, which we ascribe to any material or extended thing, from the universe, which Spinoza called God under the attribute of extension, down to the smallest imaginable particle, is not really in that thing itself; it is only in the mind of the observer to whom what is in truth infinitely *many* happens to look *one*. In souls, however, which are not extended in space, and cannot be said, except in an inexact metaphorical sense, to have parts, we find a more genuine sort of unity. Leibniz, therefore, supposes that all real individuals have a unity of this kind, though it is only some among them that we call by this name. Such individuals— he called them all 'monads', that is 'unities'—are the only things that really exist. What we call bodies— material or extended things—are proved by their infinite divisibility not to be real; for you can never come to any real components of them; there are no physical 'atoms' or indivisible particles, as Democritus in antiquity and some philosophers in modern times had supposed. What is material or extended is only a *phenomenon* or appearance; some things *look* material or extended, but are not really so in themselves. In themselves, they have the same kind of unity that a soul has. They are not always, indeed, conscious of themselves; but neither, after all, is a soul. That I think, as Descartes said, proves that I exist; but when I am not thinking, or am asleep and dreaming, or even in a dreamless slumber, my soul—that in me which thinks—does not cease to exist. If it did, there would not be the continuity which there is between my waking and my sleeping states. I should not wake at the sixth stroke of a clock when the first five had failed to wake me; I should not be refreshed for renewed thinking after a dreamless sleep. Leibniz believed that there were always what he called 'little perceptions' going on in our souls even when we are not what we call conscious at all; and here he was a pioneer in calling attention to the evidences of the existence of a mental life 'below the threshold of consciousness', as the modern phrase goes, which has become so important in modern psychology.

We may think, then, of 'monads' which are what our souls would be, if we felt but never reasoned; of others which are what our souls would be, if we were always asleep and dreaming; of others which are what our souls would be, if they were always in a sleep unbroken by dreams; and in this way can understand how to what appear to us as the bodies of animals and of plants, and even as bodies which we should not call living bodies at all, there may correspond real individual beings, all of the same nature, but not of the same capacity, as our own souls. These monads which make up the universe are not by Leibniz regarded as being acted upon by one another; for this would impair the perfect independence of each, and we should have taken a step in the direction of Spinoza's one sole independent being or substance. Whatever happens to each monad is, on the contrary, the necessary outcome of its own nature; at every moment 'it carries its whole future in its womb'. This complete mutual independence of the monads is expressed by saying that 'they have no windows by which anything can come in or go out'. But among these mutually independent monads there exists a 'pre-established harmony'; the development of each so corresponds with that of every other as to produce the appearance of an intercommunication between them which does not really take place. The relation of a man's soul to his body (which is the appearance of a number of monads less highly developed than his soul) is a particular case of this harmony, and can be compared, as by the Occasionalists, to the relation between two clocks wound up to keep time together. Owing to the 'pre-established harmony', each monad may be said to reflect the whole universe from one particular point of view out of an infinite number, from every one of which some monad reflects it. Such is, in outline, the theory by which Leibniz endeavours not only to reconcile the genuine individuality of human souls with a single universal order, but to find at every point throughout that order an individuality no less genuine, though sometimes less highly developed, than that which we know to exist in ourselves.

The universal order or harmony itself Leibniz holds to be chosen by God (of whom he sometimes speaks as of a supreme Monad from which the rest proceed) out of an infinite number of possibilities as the best possible. For Leibniz did not think with Spinoza that philosophy could dispense altogether with 'final causes'. Some things are true as matters of fact which cannot be shown to be mathematically or logically necessary. Yet it would be to give up the very presupposition of philosophy to suppose that there is no reason at all for their being as they are. Leibniz thus holds that, beside the principles of logic and mathematics, there is a 'principle of sufficient reason' according to which, if our knowledge were adequate (which it often is not), we could show that what, as we say, just happens to be thus, is better thus than otherwise. The constitution of the actual world is a matter of fact which cannot be shown to be logically necessary. It must, therefore, be explained as due to the choice of God. When Leibniz calls the world 'the best of all possible worlds' he does not mean that everything in it is, when taken by itself, as good as we can possibly imagine it to be, but only that what is, taken by itself, bad could not have been better except in a world which on the whole would have been a worse world. Thus, moral evil could not be wholly excluded from a world where there were free agents; but it is better that there should be free agents who sometimes do wrong than that there should be no free agents, and therefore no vice, but also no virtue.

The expression, however, 'the best of all possible worlds', lent itself easily to ridicule, and the theory that this world was such was held up to very exquisite ridicule by the great French wit, Voltaire, in his romance called *Candide* (1757). Followed by the most enlightened men of his nation, which was regarded in the eighteenth century as the most cultivated in Europe, Voltaire turned aside from the philosophies which, like those we have in this chapter been considering, were confident in the power of human reason to discover from its own resources the inner nature of reality, to an English philosopher, who, with a humbler estimate of the capacity of the understanding, had not, indeed, pretended to the possession of such great intellectual wealth as his French and German contemporaries, but had a more assured enjoyment of the modest estate which was all to which he had laid claim. This philosopher was John Locke.

CHAPTER VIII

LOCKE AND HIS SUCCESSORS

JOHN LOCKE (1632–1704), in his *Essay concerning Human Understanding* (1690), followed Descartes, whose writings first 'gave him a relish of philosophical things', in thinking of matter and mind as two sorts of substances which agreed in owing their being to a Deity whose existence could be rationally demonstrated; although Locke relies less upon the 'ontological argument' of Descartes as a proof of it, than upon the consideration that since *something* cannot be conceived to come from *nothing*, *something* must have existed from eternity, 'powerful' enough and 'knowing' enough to be the source of all the energy and of all the knowledge that we actually find in the world.

But Locke is less concerned than Descartes with those difficulties arising from the apparently intimate interaction of the material and spiritual substances in ourselves which had led the Cartesians to Occasionalism. In the first place, he is not so firmly convinced that each of them is just what the other is not. He does not see why God should not, had he so pleased, have endowed matter with the power of thinking; although he does not consider it at all probable that what thinks *in us* is material. He does not question that, in perception, our minds are somehow affected by the transmission to our brains of motions set up by the contact with our own of bodies external to ours. That in our voluntary actions thought has the power of exciting motion he holds to be undeniable, although incomprehensible. But his chief divergence from Descartes is in his doctrine that there are no 'innate ideas', but that all our knowledge is derived from *experience*.

Experience, he says, is of two kinds: the one being *sensation*, and the other the *reflection* of the mind 'on its own operations within itself', which may be called an 'internal sense'. Until one or the other of these has taken place, the mind is like a sheet of blank paper before anything has been written upon it. It was an easy task for Locke to show that children and savages are not from the first familiar with such general principles of reasoning as that it is impossible for the same thing at once to be and not to be this or that. But few of those who have defended the existence of innate principles and ideas have meant to assert this. They have meant rather that the 'principle of contra-diction', for instance (though, of course, not expressed in this general form), is yet *used* as soon as men begin to reason at all. *As a general principle*, it is no doubt obtained from reflection on the 'operations of the mind within itself', which is one of the two kinds of experience recognized by Locke. But the operation itself must take place in the mind before it can be thus experienced. And so Leibniz, who wrote a large work (not published till long after its writer's death), the *Nouveaux Essais*, in which he criticized Locke's *Essay* chapter by chapter, observed that, to an old saying with which Locke seemed to agree, 'that there is nothing in the understanding which was not first in the senses', one exception must be made, namely, the understanding itself.

But whatever be the case with our knowledge of the

operations of our minds, is not our knowledge of the material world wholly derived from experience by way of sensation?

'Sensations' are counted by Locke among 'ideas'; and an 'idea' he defines (in words nearly the same as those which Descartes had used) as 'whatsoever is the object of the mind when a man thinks'. But, although, according to Locke, 'ideas' are never *born in* the mind, they are always perceived by the mind *in itself*; and hence they are not what are commonly meant by 'real objects'; on the contrary, we may ask how we come to know that there *are* 'real objects' of the nature of bodies beyond the mind, which *cause* 'ideas of sensation' in us, and of whose existence and nature they inform us. Even to ask these questions, however, we must have *already* in us (whether strictly speaking, *born* in us or no) the notions of a *cause* and of bodies existing outside of one another in space. Of the origin of such notions, without which it would seem impossible to obtain from our sensations any knowledge of an external world, it is now very generally admitted that Locke was unsuccessful in giving a consistent account. Yet he had no intention of denying the independent existence of an external world: although, like Descartes, he held our knowledge of it to be less certain than the *intuitive* knowledge which each of us has of his own existence, and than the *demonstrative* knowledge we all may have of God's. He shared the view, which had become general among the thinkers of his generation, that there existed a material world, really possessed of the qualities (such as extension, shape, motion), interesting to mathematical and mechanical science, but whose apparent qualities of colour, resonance, taste, and the like were no more than feelings produced in minds by (or on occasion of) the action of the real bodies upon our organs of sense. But holding, as he did, that all our knowledge of the material world came from experience in the form of sensation, he could neither, with the ancients, distinguish the reality which reason could directly apprehend from that which only *appeared* to the senses, nor yet, with Descartes and his school, distinguish the knowledge due to ideas innate in the mind from that due to ideas afterwards produced in it consequently on an affection of the bodily organs. He, therefore, is driven to distinguish what he called the 'primary qualities of bodies', viz., those susceptible of treatment by mathematical and mechanical science, which he enumerates as follows: solidity, extension, figure, motion or rest, and number—as those of our ideas which are resemblances of patterns existing in the bodies themselves, from the 'secondary qualities'—colours, sounds, tastes, and the like—our ideas of which have no resemblance at all to what causes them in the bodies, namely the bulk, figure, and motion—the primary qualities, that is—of the minute and insensible parts of those bodies.

We may here call to mind that Bacon had hoped great things for the understanding and conquest of nature from a revival of the old Atomists' way of regarding bodies as composed of such minute and insensible parts. Such a revival had already taken place by the time of Locke in connexion with the attempts to explain all natural phenomena, so far as possible, on mechanical principles. The Frenchman Pierre Gassendi (1592–1655), a friend of Hobbes and

Descartes, had come forward as the restorer of the atomistic philosophy of Epicureanism; and the Englishman Ralph Cudworth (1617–88), under the roof of whose daughter, Lady Masham, Locke died, had represented atomism as the best system on which to explain all processes not involving vital phenomena; though both thinkers had denied any necessary connexion between atomism and the atheism which was traditionally associated with it. Hobbes and Descartes also, though, with Bacon, not accepting atomism in the strict sense of the word, had viewed bodies as composed of insensible, though not intrinsically *indivisible*, corpuscles or minute bodies; and Locke's close friend, the great chemist Robert Boyle (1627–91), had shown the practical utility of such a theory in the investigation of natural processes.

It was Locke's way of distinguishing the primary qualities of bodies from the secondary that exposed him (though not in his lifetime) to the criticism of George Berkeley (*b.* 1685, *d.*, as Bishop of Cloyne in Ireland, 1753).

It is noticeable that, of the three great British philosophers who, as we shall see, contributed one after the other to the working out to its consequences of the theory that our knowledge of the external world is derived wholly from sensation, the English, Irish, and Scottish nations can each claim one. Locke was a typical Englishman in his practical good sense, his modesty in speculation, his neglect of system, his carelessness of consistency, his avoidance of extremes. His philosophical work is of a piece with his public career as the friend and counsellor of the statesmen to whom was due the settlement of 1688, which established monarchy by a parliamentary title. Berkeley, though not of pure Irish descent, was no bad representative of his native country in his personal brilliancy and charm and in his enthusiasm for projects less practicable than attractive—such as the foundation of a great missionary college at Bermuda for the education of the children of the planters and Indians in the American colonies; or, later in his life, the curing of all the ills that flesh is heir to by tar water. In philosophy, also, he was less influenced than Locke by the habits of thought prevalent among physicists and chemists, more thoroughgoing in consistency with himself; less chary of paradox, more adventurous in speculation.

Berkeley followed Locke in holding that all our knowledge of what we call the external world is derived from 'ideas of sensation'. But he did not see what need there was to suppose anything in the way of a material substance beside these ideas, such as Locke had agreed with Descartes and most other philosophers in holding to exist, and to cause or occasion the production of ideas in us. Of such a substance, it seemed to Berkeley that it was impossible to form any conception. It was not supposed to be something which could itself be perceived; for whatever was perceived was an *idea*, and this was held to be quite different in its nature from any idea. Nor was it something which could itself perceive, like our own minds. Of these Berkeley allowed that we have a *notion*, though not, properly speaking, an *idea*. For while I never perceive my mind itself, as distinct from some particular feeling or sensation in it, yet every such feeling or sensation is something which *I* feel,

and so I am aware of myself along with every idea I
have, as having it. But the 'material substance' was
not supposed to be thus itself conscious; on the
contrary, it was just as not being such that it was
distinguished from what was regarded as the other
kind of substance, mind or spirit.

What, then, are we to suppose it to be? Locke had,
indeed, said that it was something solid or consisting
of solid parts, extended, figured, capable of motion—
but not coloured, or resonant, or odorous. But how,
Berkeley asked, could we, on Locke's own showing,
know this? How, where we have no acquaintance
with this supposed source of our ideas except by means
of them, can we tell that some of them resemble it,
and others do not? Again, it is supposed to be something of quite a different nature from an 'idea'; it is
something which cannot be perceived except by means
of an 'idea', while an 'idea' is defined as what can
be perceived. How, then, can an idea resemble it?

Lastly, even if we could suppose this difficulty got
over, and imagine the substance as resembling our
idea of a solid extended body, could we imagine it
apart from some such qualities as it is said not to
possess—from colour if we imagine it as seen,
temperature if we imagine it as touched?

Berkeley's conclusion is the rejection as inconsistent
with Locke's doctrine that we only know of bodies
what we experience of them in sensation, of the
doctrine, in which Locke followed other philosophers,
that there existed independently of our perceptions a
'material substance' which caused those perceptions,
but was not itself perceived. Of this 'denial of the
existence of matter', for which Berkeley became

famous, we are told by Boswell that Dr. Johnson said, 'striking his foot with mighty force against a large stone, till he rebounded from it, "I refute it thus!"' This, however, showed a misunderstanding of Berkeley, who intended to deny nothing to which the senses bear witness, but only the existence of something imperceptible by the senses, underlying what we actually perceive.

In saying that what we perceive with our senses is no other than the real object and not something else which represents it, Berkeley agrees with common sense; but when he goes on to pronounce that the very being of everything that is so perceived lies in being perceived, we are at once disposed to ask: What, then, becomes of it when it is not being perceived? Berkeley's reply would be that, if it is not being perceived by any conscious being or (as he says) spirit, it cannot exist, for, if we ask ourselves what we really mean by its existence, we shall always find that we mean its existence as an object of perception; and, if we imagine it existing unperceived, we are in truth only imagining it perceived without framing an idea of the person perceiving it. Such an idea, which we frame at will, is what we call an idea of imagination; but there are many ideas which are not so framed at will, which are 'more strong, lively, and distinct' than these, 'and which have a steadiness, order and coherence, and are not excited at random, as those which are the effects of human wills often are, but in a regular train or series'. These we call 'ideas of sense'.

As we cannot ourselves produce such at will in ourselves (and still less in other beings like ourselves), and as the supposition of an unthinking or unperceiving 'material substance' has been found to be unintelligible, we can only attribute their production to a thinking being or Spirit more powerful than ourselves, whose wisdom and benevolence is sufficiently proved by the 'admirable connexion' of these ideas according to what we call the laws of nature. We cannot, indeed, discover any necessity in this connexion, 'without which we should all be in uncertainty and confusion, and a grown man no more know how to manage himself in the affairs of life than an infant just born'. It is only by experience that we learn what it is; and it is only by a convenient looseness of language that we describe it by calling one idea the cause of another— fire, for example, of warmth. An idea is nothing but a perception; it is meaningless to attribute to it power or activity. The only active beings we have any reason to suppose exist are *spirits*. We are spirits, and in a measure active, as our power of forming ideas of imagination shows; and it is reasonable to suppose ideas of sense produced in us by a being of like but higher nature. These ideas of sense (which constitute what we call the external world) may thus be regarded as words of a 'divine language' by which this greater Spirit communicates with ourselves.

Without stopping to inquire whether there may not be some weak places in this reasoning, we must now point out that to Berkeley the principle of Locke that all our knowledge of bodies comes through sensation was welcome because, as we have seen, he held that, when more consistently worked out than it had been by Locke himself, it removed all ground for belief in a material substance, existing on its own account in independence of a mind perceiving it. If, however, we have no ground for such a belief, we shall not attribute the order and system which we observe in our experience to any necessary connexion between the parts or movements of such a substance, but rather to the only principle of order whereof we have any direct knowledge, namely, the will of an intelligent being. The tendency, which Berkeley observed prevalent in his day, to dispense with a God or at least, like Spinoza, to conceive his nature as capable of being expressed in terms of a material system, could thus be shown not only to be no necessary inference from the fashionable philosophy of Locke (who, indeed, had not drawn it himself), but to be actually inconsistent with that philosophy.

But Berkeley was to be treated in his turn as he had treated Locke—by David Hume (1711–76), famous for his *History of England* as well as for his philosophy, the Scotsman of the triad of British thinkers mentioned above. There was, perhaps, in Locke too much of the English lover of compromise, in Berkeley too much of the Irish visionary, to fit either the one or the other for the work which the acute intellect and sober temperament of their Scottish follower was to accomplish in bringing to light the extreme issues of the sensationalist theory of knowledge propounded by Locke. This he did in his *Treatise of Human Nature*, which 'fell dead born from the Press' in 1739.

In this work, he observed that arguments of the same kind as those by which Berkeley had proved the assumption of a 'material substance' distinct from our ideas to be needless and unintelligible, might be turned also against the 'spiritual substance' which Berkeley had retained. For what do we know of this either, except the perceptions which it is said to 'have'? And if (with Berkeley) we do not distinguish the things which we perceive from the perceptions themselves, does the theory that the 'ideas' (and therefore the 'things') are modifications of a spiritual substance, that of the soul, differ greatly from the 'hideous hypothesis' of Spinoza that all things are modifications of one substance? Yet this hypothesis is execrated by the very people who are ready to accept the kindred doctrine of a substantial soul. In truth, we know of nothing entitled, as existing on its own account, to be called 'substance' except individual perceptions. The connexion between these is (as Berkeley had said) purely arbitrary, and can only be learned from experience. Hume did not follow Berkeley, however, in thinking that this connexion could be made more intelligible by ascribing it to the will of God; for the will, in his judgement, 'has no more a discoverable connexion with its effects than any material cause'. The only discoverable connexion of any cause with its effect is that which consists in the perception (Hume calls it 'impression') or idea of one object determining us to form the idea of another, in consequence of a constant experience in which the perception or impression of the latter has been invariably found to follow on that of the former.

The upshot of Hume's discussions is a complete scepticism. Locke's denial that there can be any knowledge except what comes from experience gained by way of separate perceptions (for the 'ideas of reflection' are described as if they were separate perceptions of an internal sense) turns out in the long run to leave no room for anything to bind together these separate perceptions into a single experience or world—no innate ideas, no external world, no mind or soul. The perceptions are, indeed, associated together; but such association is mere matter of fact. The necessity which seems to belong to some connexions is only a habit of ours, not any quality of things independently of our perception. When Hume, some years later, published an *Enquiry concerning Human Understanding* in a series of essays, in which his philosophical views were expressed less trenchantly and in a less continuous and concentrated form than in the *Treatise*, he omitted his explicit reasonings against the doctrine of a substantial soul. This was partly done, no doubt, in order to secure a better hearing; but he may also himself have felt uneasy about a denial which it was impossible not to seem to contradict at every other word by speaking of 'we', of 'the mind', of 'the understanding'. Was not Descartes perhaps right in saying we could not doubt the existence of the self that doubts? But while leaving in the background in his *Enquiry* what might appear the most extravagant detail of his scepticism, Hume comes forward still as a defender of 'the Academical or sceptical philosophy'.

CHAPTER IX

KANT AND HIS CONTEMPORARIES

THE little space at our disposal makes it impossible to
find room for an account of Thomas Reid (1710–96)
and others of Hume's fellow-Scotsmen, who endeavoured to meet their countryman's scepticism by
going back to the reassertion, under the name of
'principles of common sense', of those 'innate ideas'
the existence of which Descartes had affirmed, but
Locke, followed by Berkeley and Hume, had denied.

We must pass at once to the great German thinker,
Immanuel Kant (born 1724, and from 1755 to his
death in 1804 a teacher in the Prussian University of
Königsberg)—himself, on the father's side, of Scottish
descent—who, according to his own statement, was
'waked from a dogmatic slumber' by the study of
Hume, and found nothing in the 'principles of common
sense' to reassure him in going to sleep again. By a
'dogmatic slumber', Kant meant an acquiescence in a
kind of philosophy which, like that of Christian Wolff
(1697–1754)—who had reduced the teaching of Leibniz,
though not quite without alteration, to a systematic
form—did not question the competence of the understanding to apprehend the nature of things as they
really are in themselves. The doubt which Hume had
thrown upon this competence, by his denial that the
connexion between cause and effect, which the natural
sciences made it their business to trace everywhere in
the external world, was anything more than a mental
habit of ours—this doubt made it, to Kant's mind,

imperative that philosophy should cease to be *dogmatic*, and become *critical*. By this he meant that, before dogmatically pronouncing what is true and what is not, it must examine our intellectual faculties, and see how far they are qualified to apprehend the real nature of things. His own philosophy was thus dubbed by himself a critical philosophy; and he gave to each of his three chief works the title of a *Critique* or Criticism of some intellectual faculty.

The first of these, which appeared in 1781, was a *Critique of Pure Reason*. In this, Kant believed himself to have effected a revolution in philosophy comparable to that effected by Copernicus in astronomy. Just as the motions of the heavenly bodies are explained by Copernicus as appearances due to our position on a moving earth, so, according to Kant, the position and extension of things in space, and the succession (or simultaneousness) of events in time, are only *phenomena* or appearances, due to the peculiar constitution of our faculties of perception. Thus, as the relation of cause and effect can only be supposed to exist where there is a succession, which is then interpreted as no casual succession, but a necessary one, Hume was right in his theory that the relation in question depends upon the nature of the mind, and not upon the nature of things as they are in themselves apart altogether from the mind which perceives them and reflects upon them. But this theory ought no more to lead to scepticism in philosophy than Copernicanism to scepticism in astronomy. It ought only to lead to a recognition of the inevitable limitations imposed by the nature of our faculties upon our knowledge of a reality, whose independent existence, however, we need not doubt, since, if it did not exist, it could not appear to us at all.

With Hume, indeed, it had led to scepticism; but this was because he supposed the part played by the mind in the acquisition of knowledge to be merely that of a passive recipient of 'impressions', so that nothing which it did itself could contribute anything to knowledge. Kant, on the other hand, held that the facts of mathematical reasoning alone were sufficient to show that the mind could produce genuine knowledge from its own resources. Counting, or the construction of imaginary figures, is the only possible way of arriving at results which are admitted to be both exactly and universally true. This they could not be were they reached from experience by means of the senses. For any perceptible things we might count could never be exactly equal to one another; no lines drawn on paper would be perfectly straight. And even if they were, how could we be so sure, as we are about our mathematical conclusions, that they will hold in all cases, not only in those now before us? Moreover, not only can the mind thus produce genuine knowledge from its own resources, but this knowledge, concerning as it does the very nature of *space* and also of *time* (to speak of which and say: This happened *before*, *after*, or *at the same time as* that, we must be able to count), is not a knowledge quite apart from our knowledge of the world of things and events. All *things* which we perceive with our senses are in space, all *events*, including our own acts of perception and thought, are in time. Hence, there can be no knowledge of the world of things and events which does not involve a knowledge which is produced by the mind from its own resources, or, as Kant put it, is *a priori*.

It was not wonderful that contemporaries of Kant should confound his doctrine that the bodies which we perceive are only *phenomena* with Berkeley's that they are our *ideas*; and, in a second edition of the *Critique of Pure Reason* (1787), Kant set himself to explain the difference. This he took to be that, while his own was a ' critical' philosophy, according to which we perceive things not as they are in themselves, but only as they appear to us, and so only *phenomena*, Berkeley's was a 'dogmatic' philosophy, which asserted that the things we perceive are in themselves just what we perceive. Moreover, Berkeley seemed to Kant to treat the perceiving mind as real, while treating the things perceived as only ideas in that mind. To Kant, the things perceived were no less real than the perceiving mind, of which we only become aware through its perception of them; *within experience*, what perceives and what is perceived are both alike real; but what either that which in the act of perception appears to us as the perceiving mind, or that which appears to us as things perceived, may be in itself, we do not and cannot know. This, in Kant's technical language, is expressed by saying that the external world is empirically real—as real as anything else in experience—but 'transcendentally'—that is, outside of experience— 'ideal'—that is, not real.

Perception then, by means of the senses, is, in Kant's view, perception of objects which, being already in space and time, are phenomena, appearances of things, not things as they are in themselves. But, holding this, Kant might have held, like Plato, that the

understanding (though not perception) was conversant
with realities; the more so, as he did not agree with
Locke in finding nothing in the understanding but
what had come into it through perception by the senses,
nor with Leibniz in holding perception by the senses
to be nothing but a confused sort of understanding.
Kant's view was, however, that the two faculties,
though quite distinct—so that one could not conceive
of the one as a form or modification of the other—yet
were so mutually interdependent that neither perception without understanding nor understanding without
perception could yield us any knowledge. Without
understanding, perception would make nothing of
what was perceived; without perception, understanding would have nothing to understand.

Thus, if we take the notion of *cause*, Hume's discussion of which had so great an influence on Kant, there
is, as Hume has shown, no 'impression' or perception
of causation, distinct from those of the two objects
which in a particular case we call 'cause' and 'effect'
respectively. The notion of such a relation between
two objects, therefore, since it is not derived from a
separate perception, must, according to both Hume
and Kant, be supplied by the mind—though, for Kant,
this does not mean that it is inapplicable to objects,
since all objects, so far as they are in space and time,
are themselves the result of the mind's activity. Such
notions as that of 'cause', without the use of which
we cannot *understand* what we perceive, Kant calls
'notions of the understanding' or 'categories'. They
originate in the understanding, but are applicable to
perceived objects; nay (and this is what Kant is
especially concerned to insist upon), they are only

applicable to such. This renders it idle, for example, to raise questions about a 'first cause' with nothing outside of itself or prior to itself; for such a cause could never be perceived as an object in space or time. Every object in space must have something outside of it, every event in time something before it; and to nothing which cannot be perceived as such an object has a notion like that of cause any possible application. We may, indeed, speak intelligibly of causes which are not as a matter of fact perceived (like the movements of an undiscovered planet, or an undetected bacillus), but not of causes which (like the agency of a spirit) could not under any circumstances be perceived by the senses.

But Kant recognizes that the human mind is never content to confine its speculations to the sphere within which the results can be verified by the senses. It is true that, when we suppose ourselves able by such speculations to reach knowledge about things as they are in themselves, we always find ourselves at a loss, puzzled by the seeming cogency of mutually contradictory arguments; for example, it is equally easy to give good reasons to prove that the world cannot have had a beginning, and to prove that it cannot but have had one. This shows that notions which, so long as we remain within the region of a 'possible experience', we may be sure will help us to increase our knowledge (for we shall not go wrong in seeking for a cause of every phenomenon in some other phenomenon), will fail us as soon as we pass beyond this region. Yet how could we go on, as we do in the natural sciences, seeking for a cause of every event, and then for a cause of that again, and so on for ever, if we did not all the while think we were at something better worth doing than asking a riddle for the solution of which one would always be passed on to some one else, without hope of arriving at the real answer? Are we not all the while sure that there is an all-embracing system, which must somehow exist as a whole, with a definite nature of its own that we are engaged in gradually tracing out?—although we cannot, it is true, picture it to ourselves, because, as pictured, it would be only something *in* the world, and not the world itself.

The thought of such a system or world, then, is, in Kant's phraseology, a 'regulative idea' and not a 'constitutive notion', that is, it directs our minds in their progressive attainment of knowledge, but does not add new facts to the knowledge attained. Kant deplored the modern degradation of the word 'idea' to mean any kind of object that the mind might have before it, and conceived himself to be returning to a use of it more like Plato's own, in using it to denote such conceptions as that just described, conceptions of something more complete and satisfactory than anything which experience can show. In their completeness, and in their superiority to the objects of perception by the senses, Kant makes his Ideas really like Plato's; but he makes them very unlike when he says that, just because they cannot be perceived by the senses, they have no right to be regarded as real objects or as representatives of such, but *merely* as 'Ideas'. Yet the *reason* cannot help forming these 'Ideas' (when our mind goes beyond understanding what we perceive with the senses, and speculates on the nature of reality as a whole, Kant calls it 'reason' instead of 'understanding'); and without them our *understanding* would lack the perpetual spur to activity provided by a goal towards which it can ever advance, but can never reach.

Of such 'Ideas', Kant recognizes three; that of a first cause, the ever-receding goal of the science of nature; that of a substantial soul, the ever-receding goal of the science of mind, which has always before it only some particular conscious state of mind; and that of an all-embracing reality, the ever-receding goal of philosophy, which, even in the extremest contrariety, such as that, emphasized by Descartes, between thought and extension, seeks a yet more fundamental unity, to which both Descartes and Kant give the name of God. The existence of God, of the Soul, and of a first cause or original event, such as is implied not only in a creation of the world, but (what touches us more nearly) in any free action, such as I can call in a genuine sense 'my own'—all these are thus by Kant declared to be problems which our reason, in virtue of its own nature, cannot but raise, but is, also in virtue of its own nature, incapable of solving. This does away with the possibility of such proofs as many had alleged for the existence of God.

All these to Kant seemed ultimately to rest upon one, the Ontological Argument already mentioned. This Kant is especially concerned to demolish. For it is the concentrated expression of confidence in the power of thought to apprehend reality as it is in itself. It is thus the very citadel of the 'dogmatic' philosophy for which Kant wished to substitute a 'critical'. That we cannot think a thing to be otherwise is for Kant no guarantee that the thing is thus apart from our thinking: for we have no reason to suppose that things are in themselves as they, owing to the constitution of our faculties, must appear to us as being: rather, if they were, it would be a strange coincidence   But, if all proofs of the existence of God, of an immortal soul, and of the freedom of the will are necessarily fallacious, no less must all disproofs be so: and these chief articles, as they were considered in Kant's time to be, of Natural Religion can be removed altogether from the sphere of *knowledge* to that of *faith*. By 'faith' Kant understood a holding of something for true on grounds sufficient to act upon but not fully to satisfy one's intelligence. To understand why Kant thought that there were grounds sufficient to act upon for holding it true that there was a God, that we are free agents, and that our souls do not perish at death, we must turn from his theory of knowledge to his theory of action or conduct.

To the *Critique of Pure Reason*, Kant added (in 1788) a *Critique of Practical Reason*. This dealt with the human will, as the former *Critique* with human perception and understanding. Human will is, according to Kant, 'practical reason'; for, so far as it is characteristically human, and not, like an animal's, merely instinctive, it always wills to do something for a *reason*, with some *end* in view. Every considered action, in being considered, is brought into connexion with some general scheme of conduct, whether as forwarding one's business, or as contributing to one's happiness, or as part of one's duty. In this last case, what is willed must, in Kant's view, be willed disinterestedly. It is the distinguishing mark of a morally good action that it is done not because it is pleasant to the doer, nor because it conduces to his profit in any way, but only because it is right, in obedience (to use Kant's technical expression) to a 'categorical imperative', that is, to a law which commands not *hypothetically*— 'if you would avoid this'; 'if you would have that'— but *unconditionally*.

Upon nothing does Kant insist more strongly than upon this unconditionally obligatory character of all genuine morality. Although implied, he thought, in the judgements of the unsophisticated conscience, he did not find it clearly understood by most writers on moral philosophy. There had been, during the seventeenth and eighteenth centuries, a great output of books on moral philosophy, especially in England. The impetus to this had been given by the desire to refute the teaching of Hobbes, which was generally (though, perhaps, not quite correctly) understood to make morality a matter of arbitrary enactment by the State. Some of his opponents, particularly the Ralph Cudworth already mentioned and Samuel Clarke (1675–1729), a friend of Newton and correspondent of Leibniz, insisted that the truths of morality were no more dependent on the mere will of God or man than those of mathematics. Others—as the third Earl of Shaftesbury (1671–1713), a pupil of Locke's, who did not agree with his tutor in rejecting 'innate ideas', and Francis Hutcheson (1694–1747), a Scottish professor— dwelt rather upon the presence of a natural capacity to discriminate by a kind of inward taste between the morally good and bad, as between the beautiful and the ugly. Hume, while agreeing with Shaftesbury and Hutcheson that our moral judgements depend upon sentiment and not upon reason, explained the sentiment

102   L

itself as arising from the satisfaction felt in the contemplation of actions which are *useful* or *agreeable*, not to the agent only, but to others or to all men. In a like spirit, his friend Adam Smith, the founder of modern political economy (1723–90), saw in our judgements that we ought to do or not to do this or that the result of sympathy with what would be our feelings were we impartial spectators of such an action in the case of another person.

In all such views Kant missed a due recognition of what he was convinced was the true characteristic of a moral judgement, namely the consciousness expressed in it of an *unconditional obligation*. With the writings of the British moralist of the preceding generation whose conception of morality was nearest akin to his own, the great theologian Joseph Butler (*b.* 1692, *d.*, as Bishop of Durham, 1752), he does not seem to have been acquainted; but, if he had been, he would certainly have held that even Butler had gone astray when, despite his insistence on the 'manifest authority' of conscience, he yet set 'reasonable self-love' by its side as a motive to action of co-ordinate rank with it. In some ways, a closer approximation to Kant's views on morality is found in the work of his contemporary Richard Price (1723–91), an English dissenting minister, whose publicly expressed sympathy with the beginnings of the French Revolution in 1789 called forth by way of reply Edmund Burke's famous *Reflections on the Revolution in France*. Probably Kant knew nothing of Price, who, indeed, like other British moralists, was far less consistent than Kant himself in allowing no motive but that of unconditional obligation to be consistent with a genuine morality. He was of one mind with Kant in making morality a matter of *reason*, rather than, with Hume and Adam Smith, of *sentiment*. So far he was a follower of his countrymen Cudworth and Clarke; but we find him also drawing a distinction between the 'speculative' and 'moral' aspects of understanding, which anticipates one of great importance in Kant's moral philosophy between 'theoretical' and 'practical' reason.

For Kant, while regarding the unconditional character of moral obligation as something only to be apprehended by *reason*, the sole faculty in us which takes for its object what is perfect or complete, yet insists upon the great interval between the apprehension of an unconditional command to be actually obeyed, and that of the unconditioned as a mere 'regulative idea', which forbids us to rest satisfied with anything conditioned by, or dependent upon something else, but never presents us with an object which is not so conditioned. To the 'practical reason', Kant assigned the 'primacy' over the 'theoretical'. In doing this, he is using language very unlike that which had hitherto been common among philosophers. Of all human activities, by far the highest, in the judgement of Aristotle, was that of knowing. Neoplatonists and Schoolmen had looked forward to the enjoyment of an immediate knowledge—a 'beatific vision'—of God as the goal of man's endeavour, to which the practice of virtue and piety did but point the way. To Spinoza, the noblest state of the human spirit was an 'intellectual love of God', produced by a sufficient knowledge of the parallel systems of matter and mind in which the divine nature revealed itself to us. It is true that the English philosophers of the school of

Locke had been inclined to dwell on the limitations of our knowledge, which were yet consistent with our knowing what our duty was, and fulfilling the purpose of our existence by doing it. But this way of looking at the matter was less common among the cultivated men of Germany in the age in which Kant grew up, an age which is often called that of 'Enlightenment', as being one in which a special value was attached to 'knowledge' and the superiority to the prejudices of the ignorant which knowledge conferred on its possessors.

Kant was, as he tells us himself, by natural disposition a seeker after knowledge; and had once looked down with contempt on the uneducated multitude who were incapable of it. But the influence of a great French writer, the prophet of modern democracy, Jean-Jacques Rousseau (1712–78), had converted him to a different view. He had come to regard the possession of knowledge as something on which a man had no right to value himself above his fellows. What alone is of intrinsic value is faithfulness to duty, which is within the reach of every man, high or low, educated or uneducated; while it is only some men whose duty includes—as Kant's own did—the pursuit and cultivation of knowledge for its own sake. It is, however, remarkable that, while Kant thus owed to Rousseau his view of the pursuit of knowledge (which is only for the few) as merely, so to say, departmental in comparison with morality, which is the business of all men alike, he did not by any means follow Rousseau in thinking of morality mainly as a sentiment. On the contrary, though living in an age in which Rousseau had made an extreme sentimentalism very popular, he went far in the opposite direction of allowing to sentiment as small a part in morality as possible. Not only did he insist that only when duty runs counter to interest and inclination can one ever be sure that it is the motive of any action; but he sometimes spoke as if an action which gave pleasure to the doer could not be done from a right motive.

This provoked the poet Schiller (1759–1805), who was a great admirer of his, to an epigram in which he laughed at the notion that one was only moral when one obeyed the law with horror. It was natural that such language should displease a poet. Whatever be the case with morality, an artist must certainly *feel* the beauty to which he gives expression. In his later writings, Kant came to deal with the nature of our judgements about beauty, which we are so far from supposing merely to state our individual preferences that we claim for them, as for our moral judgements, universal assent, and think, if others disagree with us, that either we or they must be wrong. Kant held that, in claiming assent for such judgements, our appeal was to a community of feeling among mankind in matters of taste. But, in claiming a like assent for our moral judgements, he thought that our appeal must lie to general principles of reason, with which feeling has nothing to do. The authority of these principles must, indeed, be recognized by the individual for himself; so far as he does not perceive in them the utterance of his own reason or conscience, but only means to some other end, such as favour with God or man, his obedience is not truly moral. Yet just because they are the utterance of his own *reason*, there can be nothing private about them. It is as a 'rational being' that he is aware of them; and every other 'rational being' must be supposed aware of them also.

It is in thus being aware of the moral law that the individual comes to be conscious of the freedom of his will; for, since he knows he *ought to* will and do certain things, he cannot doubt that he *can* will them and (so far as his will is not thwarted) do them. From this consciousness of the moral law and of the freedom which it implies, follows the recognition of the equal freedom of every other rational being who has the same consciousness; and from this, again, the thought of a commonwealth or kingdom of rational beings, bound together by their consciousness of obligation to keep the same law. There is a remarkable correspondence between these three aspects of our consciousness of right and wrong, and the three principles of Liberty, Equality, and Fraternity, proclaimed in the watchword of the French Revolution, the beginning of which Kant hailed no less enthusiastically than his English contemporary Price, and which aimed at giving a political expression to the fundamental factors recognized by him in the moral nature of man. In that freedom of the will which morality implies, Kant recognized that same idea of an unconditioned origin which to the 'theoretical reason' had presented an inevitable but insoluble problem; to the 'practical reason' it is more than a 'problem', it is a 'postulate'; for one is bound *to act as though* one were free. Yet an act, as an event in time, cannot *look* free, when surveyed from without, either by others than the doer, or by the doer himself after the act is done. Like any other event, it must have antecedents, among which the same principle as elsewhere governs our scientific study of events constrains us to search for a cause, and, even though we do not succeed in finding it, to assume it to be there. As *phenomena*, then, our actions are determined, even though they are done—and could only be done—under the idea of freedom. Kant's doctrine of freedom may be thought rather to state than to solve the difficulty. It is characteristic of a thinker in whom the moral and the scientific consciousness were alike developed in no ordinary degree that he should have refused to sacrifice either of them to the other, by treating as an illusion the consciousness of freedom without which our whole moral life would be rendered meaningless, or by pretending that as a scientific spectator one could satisfy oneself of the absolute originality of any event in time. If he tends to regard the moral consciousness as nearer to the inner nature of reality than the scientific, this may be justified by the consideration that the former is bound up with the *actual doing* of that which only comes before the latter as *already done*.

We can now see how, in the case of the freedom of the will, Kant could say that we had grounds for holding it to be true, which were sufficient to act upon, but insufficient to remove speculative doubt. He said the same of 'immortality' and of 'God'. We are conscious of an unconditional obligation to act *as though* there were before us a prospect of perpetually advancing toward an ideal which we cannot imagine ourselves having attained; and *as though* there were a ruler of the world, in whose government of it morality was the supreme consideration. No scientific investigation could turn for us these 'postulates' of practical reason into ascertained facts; for neither of them could be perceived as events in time or objects in space. But, for the same reason, neither can scientific investigation disprove them. They, along with freedom, are objects, not of knowledge, but of faith.

In his *Critique of Pure Reason*, Kant had contended that the real nature whether of the world or of the mind as they are in themselves must necessarily be unknown to us; we can only know them as they appear to us; and, though we cannot help speculating on what they are in themselves, such speculations do not admit of being brought to the only possible test, that of experience. In his *Critique of Practical Reason*, he had urged that, notwithstanding this, it is incumbent upon us to *act as though* the inner nature of things were what we had thus been led to guess it to be; although our actions, when once done, cannot *appear* to us as what, in order to do them, we had to suppose they could be, namely, the effects of our own free will. In the third and last *Critique*, which (for reasons to explain which would require a fuller account of his technical phraseology than is here possible) he called the *Critique of the Faculty of Judgement*, he discovers certain *appearances* or *phenomena* which, even as such, we cannot describe apart from that notion of a 'final cause', 'end', or 'purpose', without which we cannot *act*, but which has no place in the mathematical and mechanical kind of explanation that is the ideal of science or *knowledge* properly so-called. These appearances are of two sorts. There are the phenomena which we call beautiful. Although we do not always, when we recognize that an object is beautiful, think of any particular end or purpose which it serves, yet we do think of it as though the beauty were no accident, but produced, like the beauty of a work of art, by an intelligence with purposes, that is, by a will. Yet here too we have only to do with feelings aroused in us by the perception of certain objects. We are not justified in attributing beauty to the objects as they exist for the scientific understanding, which can, indeed, often explain the origin of beautiful things on mechanical principles, without any reference to their beauty. The other sort of phenomena which we seem unable to describe without reference to an end or purpose are organic beings, like plants and animals. Though even with these we should push mechanical explanation as far as it will go, yet there must always be something in them—the adaptation of their parts to the purposes of the whole organism—which cannot be thus explained. Here too, however, we are only to say that we cannot explain the nature of these objects without introducing the supposition of a design; we are not justified in asserting that the phenomena we thus explain could not otherwise have come into existence.

The work of Kant made an epoch in philosophy. In it lines of thought which men had long been pursuing were shown to tend, if carried out, to results more destructive than had been foreseen by those who started them. This was the case with that which originated with the abandonment by Descartes of the old acquiescence in the view that the mind could apprehend a reality which existed independently of being apprehended. The only conviction which Descartes' doubt had spared was that of the existence of his own thought. But, by means of his 'ontological argument for the existence of God' as implied in the very nature of this thought, he believed himself to have recovered all that

was worth having of what he had provisionally aban-
doned. Kant denied that there could be one among
our ideas endowed with the singular prerogative of
certifying the existence of a corresponding reality,
and thereby destroyed the bridge which Descartes
had built between the mind and the real world.
Henceforth, if Kant was right, the only world accessible
to our minds was a world of phenomena.

Again, the school of Locke had been inclined to
assume that whatever in our knowledge could be
shown to be the work of the mind, was thereby shown
not to belong to reality; and Kant had found that in
every possible object of our experience some 'work
of the mind' was involved. Thus, we could not,
indeed, say that notions like those of cause, because
they originated in the mind, must be inapplicable to
objects; but, on the other hand, in saying this we had
to allow that these objects were not things in themselves, but only phenomena.

It seemed to many that Kant had done in the sphere
of thought what the French Revolution had done in
the sphere of politics. He had brought down the
long tottering edifice of the established order, and had
made a new start possible by clearing the ground once
for all of an inveterate growth of old pretensions to
transcend the common lot of man. He had called
upon the reason to take stock of its native powers and
of the means at its disposal, before taking up once
more, with less ambition but better prospects, the
task in which the lack of any such progress toward
agreement as was exhibited by the mathematical and
physical sciences proved philosophy to have hitherto
signally failed.

CHAPTER X

THE SUCCESSORS OF KANT

As a result of the impetus given by Kant, we find during the following period a greater activity of philosophical speculation in Germany than anywhere else in Europe. Just as in France, the native land of the political revolution of the age, the old régime before the revolution came all at once to seem vastly remote, and to have scarcely anything to do with the controversies of the present, so it was in Germany, the native land of the contemporary philosophical revolution, with respect to the days before Kant. Though this was not the case elsewhere, yet on European philosophy in general the effect of Kant's work has been so great that it is scarcely an exaggeration to say that all roads in the thought of to-day lead back to him.

In dealing, therefore, with the philosophy of the nineteenth century, to which we are still too near to see it in its true perspective, and for even as full a treatment of which as we have been able to give to the philosophy of earlier times the few pages still left us are insufficient, it will be convenient to confine ourselves to describing the different ways in which some of the most prominent thinkers have worked out or criticized the various suggestions to be found in Kant. Many important names must go unmentioned; and we will stop short of the mention of any writers who are still living.

Perhaps, of Kant's doctrines, the most striking on a first impression, if also perhaps the least fruitful, is that which denies to the mind an access to ultimate reality, and limits it to a knowledge of *phenomena*. This thought was the basis of the 'positivism' of the French philosopher Auguste Comte (1798–1857), who went so far as to limit the possible range of human science to external phenomena (thus ruling out psychology), and to those within the solar system (thus ruling out sidereal astronomy). The same thought underlay also the theory of the 'relativity of knowledge' taught by the Scottish professor Sir William Hamilton (1788–1856) and his follower, the English divine and Dean of St. Paul's, Henry Longueville Mansel (1820–71), and after them, in a book called *First Principles*, by a very influential thinker, Herbert Spencer (1820–1903), who, however, differed from Hamilton and still more from Mansel in having no wish, by insisting on the limitations of knowledge, to leave room for faith in a supernatural revelation. It is noticeable that our inability to apprehend reality as it is in itself is regarded by these writers less as a defect due to the peculiar nature of our faculties than as a characteristic of all knowledge, which must always consist in a relation between a knowing mind, or 'subject', and an 'object' known. It certainly seems undeniable that one cannot know anything outside of this relation; but the question may still be raised whether a thing as known must necessarily differ from a thing as it is independently of being known.

By all the writers to whom I have just referred, their doctrine of the limitations of our knowledge was regarded as excluding the possibility of any knowledge of *the Absolute*. *The Absolute* was often mentioned in the systems of German philosophy which were put forward during the half century which followed the appearance of Kant's *Critique of Pure Reason*. The word 'absolute' has two meanings, which have not unfrequently been confused together. It may mean what is *out of relation*, and it is clear that no object of knowledge can be out of relation to the mind that knows it. It may also mean what is *perfect* or *complete*. In this latter sense, it was applied to the ultimate unity within which the two factors of knowledge, the knowing mind or subject' and the known 'object', must, just because they are thus related to each other, be both embraced. Though it may seem paradoxical to speak of this unity as if it were itself a known object, and so one of its own factors, yet in reflecting, as Kant calls upon philosophers to do, upon the nature of knowledge itself, we find that we are as a matter of fact considering it, and a name for it seems to be required.

We have seen that, according to Kant, there is, behind the phenomena which are all that we can know, what he sometimes calls 'the thing as it is in itself', but sometimes describes as a *noumenon*—that is, something of which we *think*, but which we do not *perceive*. This is what would be left if you could strip an object of all the characteristics which are due to our way of perceiving it and which make it a phenomenon; it is something which we cannot help thinking is there, and which yet can never be perceived by us as it is in itself. It is not to be wondered at that Kant should have followers who thought his philosophy would be improved by frankly recognizing that this 'thing in itself' was itself, after all, only a creature of the mind; that to suppose there need be anything in our experience which is not produced by the mind from its own resources is only an inconsistent relic of that 'dogmatic' way of thinking, of which it had been Kant's great aim to get rid.

This step was taken by Johann Gottlieb Fichte (1762–1814), who was famous not only as a philosopher, but as one of the patriots who did most to rouse the Germans to stand up for their national independence against Napoleon. Both that which knows, and that from which the knowing self in knowledge distinguishes itself and considers as its object, are regarded by Fichte as alike wholly the result of the activity of that mind to which Kant had already traced everything in our experience except what belonged to the 'thing-in-itself'. This was not, of course, your mind or mine—or rather it was no more your mind than mine, nor mine than yours. Neither in his account of knowledge, nor in his account of will, did Kant take it to be due to anything which varies from individual to individual that an object is what it must be to be perceptible or intelligible, or that a voluntary action is good. Nor, indeed, do we ever suppose, when we are counting or drawing conclusions from premises, that any other way of counting or reasoning is open to us than is open to others. Although it may be a private motive that leads me to count or to reason, an intrusion of private considerations into the processes themselves could only vitiate them. So, too, I can only judge what it is right to do by discounting any private interests and inclinations. The 'absolute self', then, which Fichte takes to be the source of all that enters into our experience, is this mind which thinks and wills in me when I think or will aright.

This is the principal difference between his view and that of Berkeley, who always speaks of external things as ideas of the individual spirits which perceive them. If we ask why the 'absolute self' always divides itself in actual experience into a self that knows and something other than the self for the self to know, Fichte, following Kant in his view that we should expect the deeper secrets of our existence to come to light in our moral rather than in our scientific experience, would answer that our moral life requires nature as an obstacle whose resistance may be overcome by effort in obedience to duty, and as a means of communication with other selves. For there must be many selves, that each self may have obligations or duties, and play its part in a moral order which is the complete expression of the absolute self; this moral order we may call God; and beside or outside of it there is no God.

To Friedrich Wilhelm Joseph von Schelling (1775–1854) it seemed that Fichte's treatment of nature as a kind of obstacle set up for the soul to exercise itself in successfully overcoming, or even as a means of communication with other souls, did insufficient justice to the spiritual significance which belonged to it in its own right, and which (as had been shown in Kant's *Critique of the Faculty of Judgement*) appears in the beauty that artistic genius discovers therein. In nature Schelling prefers to see a manifestation of the Absolute parallel rather than subordinate to its manifestation in mind; a view which recalls Spinoza's one Substance with its two attributes of extension and thought. But this correction of a one-sidedness in the system of Fichte led to the representation of the Absolute itself as something which was neither what nature was, nor yet what mind was; as though, while it was the ultimate reality underlying both, it were itself destitute of any definite characteristics.

In the words of Georg Wilhelm Friedrich Hegel (1770–1831), who, after being a fellow-worker of Schelling's in his philosophical investigations, became very critical of the results which his colleague reached, such an Absolute was like 'a night in which all cows were black'. The glance of 'intellectual intuition' by which the philosopher was supposed by Schelling to apprehend, all at once, this ultimate unity was represented as if it were something quite apart from the laborious process of reflection which had to be used in tracing out in detail the structure either of nature or of mind. It was just here that Hegel's view diverged from Schelling's. To Hegel, the task of philosophy could not be considered as complete until it was shown that, in tracing the actual structure of mind and of nature, we were tracing out the structure of the Absolute itself. The Absolute was not something which remains in the background, indifferent to its manifestations, only to be detected by some sudden flash of insight; it must rather be held to live and move and have its very being in its manifestations, so that only through the laborious investigation of these can it reveal itself to us as it is.

Such a view, Hegel thought, had been long ago suggested by the Christian doctrine of the Trinity, which represented it as belonging to the innermost nature of the supreme reality that it should manifest itself. Nor did Hegel, like Schelling, regard 'nature' and 'mind' as parallel manifestations of a single Absolute, which itself was neither 'nature' nor 'mind'.

He preferred to see in them integral parts of one process of self-manifestation, apart from which there was
no Absolute at all. Mind or spirit needed—so far
Hegel agreed with Fichte—an external world, in
striving to know and use which it might develop its
own capacities; but the external world only serves this
purpose because it sets before the mind as an object
for its study and appropriation a nature which is, in
truth, the mind's own. Kant had explained the
possibility of a scientific explanation of nature by the
presence in it of principles native to the mind (such as
space, time, causality). But he had gone wrong, in
Hegel's judgement, when he went on to speak as
though these principles were merely added, as it were,
by the mind to things which remained in themselves
unaffected by them. Were it so, our science would be
an illusion, and not a genuine apprehension of reality
at all. But it is such a genuine apprehension, since
what appears to us, the phenomenon, is the reality
appearing; the reality is not something *else* which
does *not* appear but remains all the time in the background unrevealed.

Kant held that what the mind finds itself constrained
to accept as rationally necessary is not on that account to
be regarded as in the last resort real; and that to
describe the real as that which the mind can understand would be an unwarrantable dogmatism. Hegel,
on the other hand, lays it down, in words very similar
to some of Plato's, that what is real is rational and what
is rational is real. Hence he did not approve of Kant's
emphatic rejection of that 'ontological argument for the
existence of God' in which Descartes and his followers
had embodied this very principle, that in the last resort

the intelligible and the real must be one. For how can we be said to understand or know anything but what is true and real? How is the real to be distinguished except by its intelligibility? Kant had said that we could no more argue from the thought of God to his existence than from the thought of dollars to their presence in one's pocket. The thought of dollars, however, is a thought of things which, if they exist at all, must be tangible and visible; only by an appeal to the senses could a supposition of their existence possibly be verified. But the thought of an ultimate reality which is rational or intelligible—for that is practically what is here meant by 'God'—is the thought of something which is certainly not perceptible by the senses. To appeal to the senses for verification here would be as unreasonable as it was proper in the case of the dollars. The only verification of which we could reasonably talk is that which is supplied by the actual progress of knowledge as, under the pressure of the questions which the mind puts to it, the world yields up one secret after another. But the whole business of putting the questions, distinguishing the answers, and seeing what new questions these answers suggest, is all carried on by the mind in the strength of the conviction which the 'ontological argument' expresses, that in thinking logically, that is, in following the law of its own nature, it is tracing out the actual structure of reality.

Now, Hegel thought that the method by which the mind proceeds is something like this. Some suggestion is fastened upon, as though it were the whole truth of the matter. Then difficulties are seen in it, and somebody brings forward an exactly opposite suggestion as an improvement. This proves to have just the same difficulties in it as the original suggestion; and it turns out that each suggestion, when taken apart from the other, in 'abstraction', as we say, is false: but that, if each is taken as the complement of the other, it is true, or rather one side of the truth. The champions of the two suggestions are like the two knights in the story who fought over the question whether the shield were of gold or silver when, really, one side was of gold and the other of silver, but each knight had only looked at one. This sort of process Hegel calls by the old Greek name of *dialectic*, because it naturally fell into the form of a controversy, whether between two combatants, or with a single thinker sustaining both parts; and Hegel thought that this kind of controversy was, as Plato held, the true method of philosophy, and must be so, because the world is really made up of reconciled opposites, and so can only be understood by contradiction followed by reconciliation. What can be more opposite than the two poles of a magnet, than right and left, up and down, past and future? Yet in each of these pairs one of the two is impossible, inconceivable, without the other.

The same principle may be illustrated from philosophy and from politics. One man is not another man; yet, as both are called men, there must be something which is neither of them, but just what both are, namely 'man'. But, if by 'man' we mean this something, and *not* either of the two men with whom we started, then this something will be just a third thing called 'man', and we shall have got no further. We have to recognize that 'universal' and 'particulars', 'man' and 'men', imply one another, and that we

cannot have one without the other. So again, it is
of no use to set up anarchy against despotism, a
freedom without rule against a rule without freedom.
You have the same evil in either case, namely, arbitrary
caprice. You cannot count upon anything and have
no security. There is no more real freedom under
anarchy than under despotism; no more real law
under despotism than under anarchy. Real freedom
is that which accepts the limitations imposed by a law
seen to be reasonable; real law is that which is accepted
by its subjects as what they see to be reasonable, and
therefore themselves will. This is, of course, what
Kant implied in saying that the moral law is only really
obeyed when it is recognized as reasonable and willed
as good by him who obeys it.

It must not, however, be supposed that Hegel
subscribed to all Kant's views on morality. On the
contrary, he fell foul of him for insisting that in morality
we were concerned only with what *ought to be*, and not
at all with what *is*; so that it might quite conceivably
be the case that the moral law, though unconditionally
obligatory, should never actually be obeyed. This
view seemed to Hegel inconsistent with his principle
that 'the real was the rational, and the rational the
real'; and all of a piece with Kant's willingness in
respect of knowledge to suppose that things might
very well not be in themselves what we cannot help
thinking that they are. To Hegel it was certain that,
though many things might when taken by themselves
be otherwise than they ought to be, yet, seen in their
context with the whole system of things, they would be
found to be balanced by corrective and compensating
circumstances, so that in the last resort what ought to

be really is, and what is, is what ought to be. Nothing less than this, Hegel thought, was implied in the faith of religion in God's providence, which, whether by just punishment or by merciful forgiveness, cancels the evils without which there would be no occasion for either justice or mercy.

Hegel called his philosophy 'absolute idealism'. 'Idealism' is an ambiguous word. Plato's philosophy is called idealism because it holds that the true nature of things is that which will be found to satisfy our intelligence rather than that which our senses perceive; Berkeley's because it holds that external things are just what the senses perceive them to be, since nothing but a mind can be conceived to exist independently of mind. The ambiguity depends upon the two meanings of the word 'idea'. But Hegel's doctrine may be called idealism in either sense. For, according to him, the world is only known aright as it reveals itself to the most patient and persistent effort to understand it; for its innermost nature is one with that of the mind; in the mind's knowledge of the world, the world knows itself, just as in knowing the world the mind knows itself. The poet Shelley has expressed this thought in words put by him into the mouth of Apollo, the personification of philosophy, the most thorough-going kind of knowledge:

> I am the eye with which the Universe
> Beholds itself and knows itself divine.

These views of Hegel's implied a very different conception of history from what many other philosophers had entertained. It was no mere catalogue of events, many of which, from a moral point of view, ought not to have taken place—which, at the best, did but illustrate general principles that might have been ascertained otherwise. To Hegel it was the actual unfolding of the nature of mind or spirit; we can trace in it an acted 'dialectic', in which particular principles are worked out, reveal their one-sidedness, drive men to oppose them, conflict with their opposites, are reconciled with them by solutions which do justice to both parties. Nor is this drama a mere idle show; only by reflection upon what is thus enacted could the mind have discovered and appropriated its meaning.

Just as Bacon's high estimate of the philosophical value of natural science had encouraged men to devote themselves to it, so Hegel's high estimate of the philosophical value of history encouraged that great movement of progress in historical study which has been one of the glories of the nineteenth century. But, like Bacon, Hegel was only helping forward a movement which had already begun. A reaction from the contempt of the past shown in the French Revolution had set in. The violent destruction of old institutions, and the contempt of national traditions, exhibited by the French in their efforts to impose by arms on all men alike a system based on rights assumed to belong to men in general, had aroused a slumbering loyalty to such institutions and traditions. Then followed a period in which, under the influence of a new enthusiasm which the French Revolution had itself stirred up, a restoration of old landmarks—though with a difference—was the order of the day. Hegel, too, in his own department was striving to build up anew the confidence in reason which Kant had shaken, and yet was availing himself in his task of the new life which Kant had put into philosophy; nor was his own system by any means a mere reproduction of those which had existed before Kant. So he became the philosophical exponent of the period of Restoration. Beyond doubt, it was an important lesson that he had to teach, that the individual mind finds itself, when it first begins to think, a member of a society, with a tradition which is the product of a wider experience, a deeper knowledge than any which the individual mind can claim; indeed, the individual mind owes to it all the thoughts of which it is as yet possessed; and, further, that no criticism of this tradition can be effective which is not preceded by a thorough appropriation of the good which is in it. But it was not surprising that established authorities should have been tempted to exploit in their own interest a philosophy so respectful toward existing fact, so severe on irresponsible criticism, so sure that right, in the long run, always has the might, and hence so easy to persuade that actual might is a proof of right. Still less surprising was it that, in the fourth decade of the nineteenth century, a philosophy which in the preceding decade had been visibly in favour with the Prussian Government should have fallen into disrepute with a generation whose discontent with such governments bore fruit in the revolutionary movements of 1848.

But, even in the heyday of the Hegelian philosophy, with its profound conviction that honest and strenuous effort to understand the world would ever be rewarded by an assurance, not otherwise to be won, of its ultimate rationality and goodness, a voice of protest was raised in Germany itself by Arthur Schopenhauer (1788–1860), who had come to the opposite conclusion that all existence is essentially evil, and that the fruit of our efforts to understand it is the knowledge of this, whereby we are saved from any more being the dupes of what he called 'the will to live'. This pessimistic philosophy, like its Hegelian opponent, could trace its descent from Kant. Kant had given to will the primacy over knowledge; had taught a freedom of the will which could yet never be the object of knowledge; had regarded space and time not as qualities of things in themselves, but as ways in which we perceive them. He had also been compelled by the facts of human nature to agree with the tradition of Christian theology that there was an original sinfulness or root of evil in the will of every man, which could not be traced to any events in his individual life. In Schopenhauer we find all these points emphasized. The will is the only reality; the faculty of knowledge is merely brought into existence to minister to its gratification; since time and space are not qualities of things in themselves, they are not qualities of the will: and since it is only by means of them that we distinguish individual things from one another, all such distinctions are merely illusory, the true reality in all being the same —namely, a radically evil will, a will or lust to live.

The only way of deliverance from the tyranny of this insatiable craving lies, according to Schopenhauer, in the lust for existence being checked, and a new path entered upon which may end in the return of the will into that state of nothingness from which it has only emerged to seek a happiness in living which living can never yield; for in all life the painful, by common consent, vastly predominates over the pleasant. Upon this path of self-renunciation and eventual salvation from itself, the will is enabled to enter by means of the reason which it brought into being as the instrument of its vain efforts after satisfaction through living. For when this reason has found out the means of satisfying the various vital desires, it does not rest, but goes on to discover the grand secret that these desires are infinite and cannot be satisfied, so that only in the abandonment of the quest of such satisfaction can salvation be found. By reaching the conclusion that all the myriad forms of life are but endless reproductions of the one will, it stills the craving for separate satisfaction in the individual who sees his individuality to be illusory. In art, it translates the struggle of life into an object of contemplation which one may behold without taking part in it or wishing to do so. Finally, in religion (which in Schopenhauer's view has nothing to do with a personal God) the vanity of existence is completely seen through, all love of phenomenal things departs, and the saint awaits in a perfect calm, such as is portrayed in the images of the Buddha (one of which stood on Schopenhauer's table beside the picture of Kant), that blessed nothingness from which no will for a separate life now divides him. The mention of the Buddha reminds us that this aspiration after a deliverance from conscious life itself as the supreme evil is one which had before Schopenhauer been more familiar to the East than to the West; and he himself was, in fact, not a little influenced by a translation of certain books of Indian philosophy, the *Upanishads*. Unlike Kant, to whom he owed so much, he did not regard the essence of a moral life as consisting in the discharge of duties towards men who have corresponding duties towards ourselves, but rather in sympathy for the suffering of one's fellows;

and animals, though they can have no duties towards us, are no less than men our fellows in suffering. In this respect, also, he was closer to the traditions of Indian than of European moral philosophy.

The high hopes of a new era of popular freedom and universal peace which were abroad from 1848 to 1852 were destined to disappointment. War followed on war in Europe; and the free progress of commerce and industry seemed to be leading less to general happiness and harmony than to misery in great cities and to fierce international competition for markets. These things helped to gain for Schopenhauer's pessimism a hearing after this date which it had never won before. His depreciation of knowledge, as compared with will, met also with ready acceptance in a generation impressed by the failure both of the systems in which Hegel and others had professed to reveal the secret of the universe, and also of the natural sciences, despite the progress they had made during the first half of the nineteenth century, to solve what Tennyson called 'the riddle of the painful earth'. The positive side of this part of Schopenhauer's philosophy, the emphasis on will, received a remarkable development at the hands of Friedrich Wilhelm Nietzsche (1844–1900), who, so to say, made Schopenhauer's devil, the 'will to live', into his god, and, instead of preaching renunciation as a means of escape from it, called for a more robust affirmation of it as a 'will to be powerful', which would imply a rejection of the morality of gentleness, pity, and resignation which Schopenhauer had agreed with Buddhism and Christianity in recommending, and which seemed to Nietzsche fit only for slaves, in favour of a morality of ruthless self-assertion, which might bring to its votaries the victory in the struggle for existence. It is thus that a higher kind of man, the 'superman', will be produced; for it is always through the 'struggle for existence' that new and more vigorous forms of life are developed. This Nietzsche had learned from the biological theory by which, in 1859, Charles Darwin (1809–82) had explained the origin of the various species of organic beings 'by means' (to quote the title of his famous book, the *Origin of Species*) 'of natural selection, or the preservation of favoured races in the struggle for life'.

The stress laid by Kant in his third *Critique* on the difficulty of accounting for organic phenomena by purely mechanical principles was an indication of the fact that the attention of students of natural science, which had in the seventeenth century been concentrated on problems of mechanics and physics, had during the eighteenth been turning towards those connected with the processes of life. This shifting of interest was bound to bring forward the notion of *development*. The outstanding facts about organisms, as contrasted with other things, are those of growth and reproduction. The production of the plant or animal from the seed or egg, though involving at every point the combination and separation of atoms or molecules, seems throughout to exhibit a tendency toward the reproduction of the parent form, which it is hard to describe except in terms of an intention or design to reproduce it. In one stage of such a process, the organism appears very different from what it does at another; yet we consider it the same organism in both stages, and describe it as it is in either of them with reference to what it has been or is to be in the other. In tracing back the history of an organism, no absolute break of continuity is to be found even at the point where, in our common way of speaking, the organism itself has been produced by another or by the union of two other organisms of the same kind; among what we regard as the lower kinds of organism it is a matter of no small difficulty to decide where a new individual life begins. It is obvious that commonly the variations between parent and offspring are confined within certain limits; it is always a plant or animal formed on the same plan as its parent that is produced from it, although it may differ in many particulars. Yet there seems to be a resemblance between some kinds which is far closer than between others; and it is often difficult to decide when two organisms are of different though closely resembling kinds, and when of different varieties of the same kind. The experience of gardeners and animal-breeders sufficiently shows that, by varying the conditions of life and breeding from selected individuals, plants or animals of very widely different appearance and habits can be obtained from the same stock. This was bound to suggest (along with other facts, such as the close likeness of the immature forms of some organisms to the mature forms of others) that the line between different kinds might itself not be impassable; that all the different kinds of plants and animals might be descended from a few ancestral stocks or even from one.

But actual evidence of the origin of one kind from another was lacking; the time usually supposed to have elapsed since the creation of the world was too short, the influence of tradition too strong—for the

Aristotelean philosophy which had moulded the scientific language of Europe had assumed a number of eternally distinct kinds, and the Bible had described an original creation of the plants and animals after their kinds—to make the suggestion seem anything but a hazardous speculation. It was otherwise when the researches of geologists had shown the earth to be far older than had been supposed, and when Darwin had suggested that, just as pigeon-fanciers or gardeners succeeded in producing very various offspring from the same stock by selecting individuals to breed, so varieties might be produced by nature on the same principle; for the survival in the struggle for existence which took place, where there was not food enough for all, of those best adapted to the environment would bring it about that in each generation it would be those of a species which had certain advantages over their fellows that would live to reproduce their kind in offspring likely to inherit in their turn any character-istic which had helped their parents to survive. Though this leaves unexplained many things which call for explanation, yet, by suggesting a possible means by which one species could have come from another, it at once brought the whole notion out of the region of mere speculation into that of scientific hypothesis; and it may to-day be considered as an accepted conclusion of natural science that what are now different species and do not breed with one another have yet originated from common ancestors, and that 'the natural selection' described by Darwin has at least been a very important factor in the process.

Philosophy had not waited for Darwin to begin thinking upon the lines suggested by biological study.

Hegel's whole philosophy, in particular, was a philoso
phy of development or evolution, since it taught tha
the discovery of the complete nature of reality, or th
Absolute, was only to be reached by tracing out
continuous series of appearances, each more comple
than its predecessors and yet involved in them, as th
complex organism is developed from the comparativel
simple germ. Although Hegel was premature i
supposing his knowledge sufficient to exhibit thi
series as fully as he professed to do, he had shown tha
the objects of experience cannot be regarded in isolatio
from one another; that, to understand the nature o
anything, it is no less necessary to understand what it i
not, than what it is; and that the utmost unlikenes
between two things does not mean that the considera
tion of them can be kept apart, any more than even
ness in numbers can be considered apart from oddnes
or curvature in lines apart from straightness. But thi
thought did not become common property unti
Darwin had convinced men that great unlikeness i
organic species was consistent with a common descent
Especially was this so in Darwin's own country, wher
the influence of German thought was for a long whil
little felt.

For the main stream of English thought at the en
of the eighteenth century and beginning of the nine
teenth had run in a channel apart from that of Con
tinental philosophy. From the days of Newton an
Locke, there had existed a tradition of friendly allianc
between devotion to the natural sciences and acceptanc
of the doctrine that our knowledge of the externa
world, with which they dealt, was wholly derived from
the senses. To admit the presence of any othe

element in that knowledge was, it was suspected, to leave room by the side of observation and experiment for what Bacon had called 'anticipations' of the facts. But it had been the lesson taught by Bacon, loyalty to whom as the national philosopher had come to be regarded almost as a point of honour, that we must never dictate to nature, but only humbly learn of her. To men trained in such a tradition, the emphasis laid by Kant and his followers on the recognition of an independent activity of the mind in every kind of knowledge was not calculated to recommend their systems. Hence, although the German philosophy of the late eighteenth and early nineteenth century exercised, especially through the poet Samuel Taylor Coleridge (1772–1834) and Thomas Carlyle (1795–1881), no inconsiderable influence on the general trend of cultivated thought in England, it was long before it came to affect to any great extent the chief representatives of scientific speculation. The principal work of these had lain in attempts to follow up a hint of Bacon's, and apply to the study of mind the methods of observation and experiment so successfully used in the study of external nature. They treated individual minds as though composed of 'ideas', much as the physicist or chemist treated bodies as composed of atoms or molecules; and endeavoured to ascertain the laws of the combination or 'association' of these ideas, upon which the various processes which occur in our mental life might be supposed to depend. In ordinary conversation 'association of ideas' is usually invoked to explain something being said or done of which no rational or logical justification can be given: but, in the theories of the thinkers with whom we are now concerned, rational connexion itself is treated as merely a particular kind of such association which is often observed to occur. Thus we have already found Hume explaining the notion of a cause as arising from an often repeated association of this kind; and, on the principles of a philosophy for which isolated perceptions are the sole ultimate constituents of knowledge, no other explanation of the facts of mind was possible.

The best known names among these 'empirical psychologists' are those of David Hartley, a contemporary of Hume (1705–57) and, in a later generation, of James Mill, the historian of British India (1773–1836), his son John Stuart Mill (1806–73), and Alexander Bain, Professor at Aberdeen (1818–1903). In the interval between Hartley and the elder Mill, two Scottish professors, Reid, who has already been mentioned, and his pupil Dugald Stewart (1753–1828), had devoted themselves to the study of the operations of the mind, without questioning the possibility of isolating them like physical processes for the purposes of observation, but also without denying to the mind the possession of principles of its own, independent of what it acquires through perception, and without supposing that 'association' was the only clue to the understanding of what takes place in it. These were the founders of what was called the Scottish school of philosophy, of which Sir William Hamilton, of whom we have already spoken, was the most eminent member. The general characteristic of this school was a confidence in the trustworthiness of the common sense and instinctive convictions of mankind, which made them the opponents of scepticism, whether as to the existence of a reality independent of our perception, or as to the

presence of a moral quality in actions independent of
their pleasantness or utility to the doer.

On the other hand, those who held that we had no
source of knowledge but sensations or feelings were
naturally disposed to see in morality nothing but
variously compounded feelings of pleasure and pain.
So arose what came to be called Utilitarianism, of
which the chief exponents were Jeremy Bentham
(1747–1832) and John Stuart Mill, and which was
defined as the doctrine that a good action is one which
conduces to the greatest happiness of the greatest
number. This was a view which recommended itself
to men whose chief interest lay in public service; and
it actually proved highly effective in promoting legal
and social reform in England. But its theoretical basis
was scarcely sufficient to support its superstructure.
The 'greatest happiness' was explained to mean the
greatest amount of pleasant feeling and least amount of
painful; and it was assumed that the pleasure of the
greatest possible number of persons could be treated
as a maximum of pleasant feeling, although not felt
as such by any individual. The principle which was
put forward as the basis of the doctrine, that a man
could desire nothing but pleasure, that is, no doubt,
his own pleasure, was reconciled with the recommenda-
tion to pursue the pleasure of others by the rule 'that
everyone was to count for one and no more than one',
a rule which seemed to appeal for acceptance to quite a
different kind of desire from one for one's own pleasure.
The principle of 'association' was called in to explain
the appearance of a love of virtue for its own sake;
a man who had learned that virtue was the best means
of obtaining pleasure might come to forget the end in

the means, as the miser comes to care for money without thought of its uses.

The theory was manifestly shifted from its original basis when John Stuart Mill, in expounding it, said that one must take account of quality in pleasure as well as quantity; for this made it plain that something could be desired in an action besides its pleasantness. But, from first to last, its defenders were opposed to any theory of an intuitive perception in actions of a moral quality independent of the production of pleasant feeling; just as they were opposed to the recognition in knowledge of an intuitive certainty of anything beyond the fact of present or past sensations. One difficulty which these views had to face was that of explaining the actual strength of conviction both as to what was right and wrong, and as to the truth of logical and mathematical axioms from an experience in each individual of the constant tendency of certain actions to produce pleasure, or of the constancy of certain results of measurement and enumeration, even when this experience was supplemented by the influence of early teaching to the same effect. A way out of this difficulty was suggested by Darwin's theory of the origin of species, which called attention to the facts of heredity, and traced the pedigree of human beings to organisms which had existed innumerable ages before the appearance of men on the earth.

The suggestion was made by Herbert Spencer that the intuitive convictions of individuals, which believers in repeated perceptions as the sole source of knowledge had found it so hard to account for, might result from the inheritance of an ancestral experience of such perceptions, going back to very remote ages. This seemed to promise a reconciliation of two opposed views of knowledge and morality which had seemed irreconcilable. But the reconciliation (even if there had not been more than a doubt of the fact of the inheritance of the results of individual reflection) was rather apparent than real. The difficulties of those who could not be satisfied with deriving knowledge and the moral consciousness from repeated perceptions were only thrown further back; and the argument that no amount of experience of this kind could justify statements absolutely universal remained precisely where it was before.

A more serious challenge to empiricism and utilitarianism came from students of Kant and Hegel, such as Thomas Hill Green of Balliol College, Oxford (1836–82), in whose judgement English philosophy since Hume had gone astray through not realizing that Hume's scepticism had shown no further progress to be possible along the lines of sensationalism, either in the study of knowledge or in that of morality. Natural science, which the empirical school of thinkers had always believed to support their views, was really, it was pointed out, inconsistent with them, since it implied the existence of objects which, though they might be felt, could not be reduced to a combination of feelings. In the same way, the assumption that a common good or happiness to be aimed at by individuals could be explained as a mere aggregate of feelings which were in their own nature momentary was, so it was argued, illegitimate. It was necessary to suppose, over and above these momentary sensations and feelings, a permanent self or mind to experience them, to remember and think of them when they are past, to treat them not merely as though, like the moments of time, each perished in turn as the next was born, but as coexisting parts of one experience. It was not contended that there were real objects independently of such a permanent self; Berkeley was right in holding that the external world only existed as an object for a mind; but the mind in question must not be a mind merely perceiving what is here and now; it must be a mind which can know what is everywhere and always true.

Now there was an ambiguity in this language, which might seem to refer either to the individual mind, which treats its successive experiences as all its own, but as none of them another individual's; or to the mind which may be said to think in each individual, and for which all individual experiences with their objects make up one real world. What was the relation of this universal mind, which Green sometimes called God, to the individual minds which were sometimes spoken of by him as its 'reproductions'? It was not wonderful that there were critics who considered that a philosophy of this kind did less than justice to individual personality either in God or in men. The criticism probably seemed less serious to those at whom it was levelled, because they were disposed to follow Hegel in thinking that the conception of one's individual self as quite separate from other individual selves was a conception which, if pressed one-sidedly, would prove, like all other conceptions, to require supplementing by the opposite thought that only in its mutual relations with other selves can a self possess an individual character, and so to lead on to the higher conception of all these mutually related selves as organs of a single mind or consciousness, operative in and through them all, which may be called divine. To others, however, this notion of a universal mind seemed a mere abstraction from particulars, like the general notion of a hand or an eye. They did not consider the difference made by the fact that the mind, when seeking knowledge, always strives to get rid of individual peculiarities and apprehend the truth as it is and as any mind that was performing its functions aright would find it to be. They, therefore, held that separate individual minds were all that had to be considered; but they shared with those they criticized the 'idealism' which could not conceive of objects existing independently of any mind. Such a view has been called 'personal idealism'.

A further extension of the tendency to assert the independence of individual minds is to be seen in the theory which, under the name of 'pragmatism', asserts that the only test of truth is to be found in its bearing upon human interests and purposes; a theory which was maintained at the beginning of the twentieth century by the American William James (1842–1910), a celebrated psychologist, and a brilliant and inspiring writer and teacher of philosophy. At a considerably earlier date, the sharp distinction drawn by Kant between the speculative and the practical reason had given birth to a distinction of 'judgements of existence' and 'judgements of value'; and religious dogmas which seemed inconsistent with the conclusions of natural science or of historical research were reckoned, as also were statements which affirmed the beauty or ugliness of objects, among 'judgements of value'; they were affirmations of what was good or bad, not of what did or did not exist in a world which was supposed indifferent to our estimate of its worth. 'Pragmatism' may be said to treat *all* judgements as 'judgements of value', and to leave none that assert a reality independent of our estimate of its worth.

It is not to be wondered at that such extreme developments of 'idealism' should be met by a movement critical of all idealism, and concerned to reassert the existence of objects independent of our perception or knowledge of them. Such a view is often called 'realism' in opposition to 'idealism'; this is, of course, quite a different sense of the word from that in which it was used in reference to medieval philosophy as the opposite to 'nominalism'. Kant himself objected to his own philosophy being called idealism and insisted that we must recognize, beside the phenomena we perceive, a 'thing in itself' which we do not perceive, and of which, therefore, we can have no positive knowledge. Nor since the time of Kant have there ever been lacking philosophers—like Johann Friedrich Herbart (1776–1841), who was a successor of Kant at Königsberg, and is celebrated as a writer on the theory of education—to maintain against the prevalent idealism the necessity of acknowledging the existence in the world of something not of the nature of mind; although the question what the nature of this something may be has been very variously answered. So great has been the influence of Kant that there have been few whole-hearted defenders of the view, which the natural sciences and common sense may be said to take for granted, that space and time belong to things as they are in themselves and not merely as perceived by us. Some who will not admit this of space have allowed it of time; among them may be mentioned a German thinker who has exercised no small influence on English-speaking students of philosophy, Hermann Lotze (1817–81).

Herbert Spencer professed to be a realist; but, while he usually thought as one, he combined with his realism the doctrine, which was Hume's, that the distinction we make between the real and the imaginary can be reduced to that between more and less vivid ideas; while in his *First Principles* he took up the position that ultimate reality is unknowable, and phenomena alone are knowable. It must be remembered that though materialism, the doctrine that matter is the sole reality, is not consistent with the 'idealism' which holds it to be of the essence of material things to be apprehended by mind, yet 'realism' need not be materialism, but may admit as alike included within one real world, both bodies, situated or moving in space and changing in time, and minds, not in space and not so wholly in time but that they can distinguish themselves from their successive states and apprehend truths to which the lapse of time makes no difference.

The thought of the nineteenth century has been dominated, though not at all times or places equally, by the conception of development or evolution, which is congenial to the biological and historical studies characteristic of the period, and which has greatly promoted their progress by introducing a principle of arrangement of which little notice had been taken in the preceding age, whose predominant scientific interest lay in the direction of physics. Hence the attraction of a programme like that of Herbert

Spencer's 'Synthetic Philosophy', which promised to show how this conception could exhibit all the complex phenomena of nature and mind, from atoms up to societies, as necessarily resulting from one simple principle, the 'persistence of force', by a continuous process, each step of which was marked by an increasing complexity, but also by an increasing coherence. Although Spencer's success in carrying out his programme may be doubted; although confusions, inconsistencies, gaps in the argument, failure to grapple with relevant questions of the greatest philosophical importance, may be plausibly alleged against him; yet it cannot be denied that it was he, more than any other thinker, who made current among the English-speaking peoples the conception of development or evolution—a conception which Spencer, indeed, carried over with too light a heart from the organic to the inorganic world, but of which the importance at least in respect of the former can hardly be overrated.

We may illustrate the difference made by it to our ways of thinking by showing that, while the eighteenth century was apt to look upon society as a contract, and forget that it differed from other contracts by the fact that it is neither made nor changed in accordance with a design deliberately formed by any individual mind, nor yet can be dissolved at the mere will of the parties, the nineteenth century came to look upon a society as an organism, and often to forget that, while it resembles an organism in its continuous change in a direction not designed by any individual member of it, but yet in accordance with ascertainable laws tending to the preservation of the type, it depends nevertheless at every moment for its existence upon the consciousness in the members of their mutual relation, and in that respect resembles a contract.

But the conception of development, which is borrowed from the sphere of organic life, requires for a final judgement upon its precise scope a clearer conception of what is meant by life than can be said as yet to have been obtained. Philosophy, always concerned to define distinctions, has before it the problem of the relation of life to mere mechanism on the one hand, and to intelligence on the other. There seems to be in life something which mechanism cannot explain, and which, as Kant said, we naturally interpret in terms of an intelligence aiming at an end; but it is exceedingly difficult to satisfy oneself where this intelligence is, whether within or without the living being concerned, and if (as to the present generation seems more probable) within it, how it can be there, as it often appears to be, without a consciousness of the end on its part. The existence and importance in our lives of processes which, while continuous with consciousness, do not seem to be themselves conscious, have been emphasized by the psychological investigations which in recent times have been so zealously undertaken; but the subject is one on which much thought must yet be bestowed before its real bearing on the great problems of philosophy can be ascertained. It is already clear that the discussion of the nature of life will pose philosophy with a new form of the old questions of the existence of matter, of the nature of individuality, of the one and the many. It may seem and has seemed, even to some philosophers, that philosophy makes no progress; that it is ever revolving the same old problems, 'ever learning and never coming to a knowledge of the truth'.

But such a view is inadequate. Philosophy does not, it is true, progress, like the sciences, by the accumulation of new facts belonging to its own special department. But the progress of the sciences is at the same time the progress of philosophy. The old problems remain, because the world remains in its structure the same; but in each generation, so far as forgetfulness of the lessons of the past does not make it necessary to go over old ground again (and the individual student must always do this in order to place himself on the level of his age), the philosopher may survey the old prospect from a point whence he can see how it lies in relation to other places which from a lower elevation were not visible together with it. We may, perhaps, carry the metaphor further, and admit that, as he goes higher and higher, some details once clear will be lost to view; and compare the study of the history of philosophy, not in a compendium like this but in the actual works of the great thinkers of the past, to a telescope whereby he may make good his loss, and enable himself to come as near as maybe to answering Plato's description of the ideal philosopher— 'the spectator of all time and of all existence'.

BIBLIOGRAPHY

THIS list of books includes only histories of philosophy; but the study of these cannot be profitably pursued apart from direct study of the principal thinkers of whom they treat.

I. GENERAL HISTORIES OF PHILOSOPHY

The History of Philosophy, by Dr. J. E. Erdmann. English translation edited by Prof. W. G. Hough, Minneapolis, U.S.A., in 3 vols. (vol. i, Ancient and Medieval; vol. ii, Modern; vol. iii, After Hegel—this last volume deals only with German philosophy). Sonnenschein, 1890–91.

A History of Philosophy from Thales to the Present Time, by Dr. F. Ueberweg. Translated by G. E. Morris, Michigan, U.S.A., in 2 vols. Hodder & Stoughton, 1885. (This is rather a book of reference than a book for reading straight through.)

Two older books, by distinguished authors, will be found interesting. *A Biographical History of Philosophy*, by G. H. Lewes, in 4 vols., 1845–46 (there are several later editions), and *Moral and Metaphysical Philosophy*, by F. D. Maurice, in 2 vols., 1872. The former is inspired by a desire to prove, in the spirit of Comte, the impossibility of philosophy as a science of ultimate reality; the latter by a desire to show that philosophy culminates in Christian theology.

As an unpretending account of the general history of philosophy on a smaller scale, *A Student's History of Philosophy*, by A. K. Rogers (Macmillan Co., 1923), may be recommended.

II. ANCIENT PHILOSOPHY

The English translations of the different sections of Dr. E. Zeller's *History of Greek Philosophy*, published by Longmans, 1868–97, under the titles *Pre-Socratic Schools*, *Socrates and the Socratic Schools*, *Plato and the Older Academy*, *Aristotle and the Earlier Peripatetics* (2 vols.), *Stoics, Epicureans and Sceptics*, *History of Eclecticism in Greek Philosophy*.

Greek Thinkers, by Theodor Gomperz. English translation. In 4 vols. Murray, 1901–12.

Greek Philosophy (Thales to Plato), by Prof. J. Burnet. Macmillan, 1914.

The Evolution of Theology in the Greek Philosophers, by Edward Caird. (Gifford Lectures.) 2 vols. MacLehose, 1904.

The Development of Greek Philosophy, by Robert Adamson. Blackwood, 1908.

The Religious Teachers of Greece, by James Adam. Clark, 1908.

III. MEDIEVAL PHILOSOPHY

History of Medieval Philosophy, by Prof. Maurice de Wulf. Translated by E. C. Messenger. 2 vols. Longmans, 1926. This work is useful as a catalogue of medieval philosophers and their writings. As a history may be mentioned, though not yet translated from the French, the excellent little book by Prof. Étienne Gilson, *La Philosophie au moyen age Le Scot Érigéne à G. d'Occam*. Payot, Paris, 1925.

IV. MODERN PHILOSOPHY

A History of Modern Philosophy, by Dr. Harold Höffding. English translation by B. E. Meyer. 2 vols. Macmillan, 1900.

The Development of Modern Philosophy, etc., by Robert Adamson. Vol. i. Blackwood, 1903.

V. SPECIAL BRANCHES

History of Materialism, by F. A. Lange. English translation by E. C. Thomas. In 3 vols. London, 1879.

The Philosophy of Religion on the Basis of its History (since Spinoza), by Dr. Otto Pfleiderer. English translation. In 4 vols. Vols. i and ii. Williams & Norgate, 1886–87.

A History of Aesthetic, by Dr. Bernard Bosanquet. Sonnenschein, 1892.

Article on 'Ethics' in *Encyclopaedia Britannica* (11th ed.), by the late Prof. Sidgwick and the Rev. H. H. Williams.

Outlines of the History of Ethics for English Readers, by Henry Sidgwick. Macmillan, 1888 (incorporating his part of the *Encycl. Brit.* article above mentioned).

Types of Ethical Theory, by James Martineau. 2 vols. Oxford, 1886.

A History of European Thought in the Nineteenth Century, by J. T. Merz. 4 vols. Blackwood, 1896–1912.

INDEX

Abelard, Peter, 96 f., 100

Absolute, the, 172 ff., 190

Academy, the (*see also* Plato), 39, 71, 151

Albertus Magnus, Count of Bollstädt, 111

Alcibiades, 20 f.

Alexander the Great, 48, 69

Alfred, King, 93

Anaxagoras, 35 ff., 67

Anaximander, 13

Anaximenes, 13

Anselm, Saint, 123

Antisthenes, 58

Archimedes, 54, 94

Aristippus, 58

Aristophanes, 16 ff., 22

Aristotle, birth, 40; student at Academy, 39, 40 f.; critic of Plato, 39, 41, 49 f., 102; logic, 40, 50 f., 94, 96 f., 102, 112; founder of Lyceum, 41; theory of Forms, 41 ff., 47, 85, 95; astronomy, 45 f., 116; idea of God, 45 f., 83, 123, 131; teleology, 46 f., 53, 71; view of knowledge, 46 f., 50, 163; works, 47 f., 93 f., 97, 108, 112; Alexander as pupil, 48, 49; idea of civilized state, 48 f.; scientific inquiry, 50 f., 56, 112 f., 189; technical language, 51 f., 119; metaphysics, 51 f., 102; attitude to Atomism, 53 f.; indictment for impiety, 67; view of ethics, 71; relation to Christian theology, 98 ff., 106; reaction against, 106, 119, 128; death, 40, 69

Arnold, Matthew, 44, 62

Atomism, 52 ff., 89, 136, 143 f.

Augustine, Saint, 77 f., 90 ff., 102, 119, 128

Averroes (Ibn Rosch), 98

Bacon, Francis, 8, 11, 27, 52 f., 110 ff., 143 f., 182, 191

Bacon, Roger, 110 f.

Bain, Alexander, 192

Bentham, Jeremy, 193

Berkeley, George, Bishop of Cloyne, 144 ff., 152, 155, 175, 181, 196

Bernard of Clairvaux, 97

Boethius, Anicius Manlius Severinus, 92 ff.

Boswell, James, 147

Boyle, Robert, 113, 144

Browning, Robert, 70

Bruno, Giordano, 116

Buddha, Buddhism, 31, 185

Burke, Edmund, 162

Burnet, John, 9

Bury, John Bagnell, 70 and n. 2

Butler, Joseph, Bishop of Durham, 162

Carlyle, Thomas, 48, 191

Cassiodorus, Magnus Aurelius, 92 f.

Categorical imperative, 161

Categories, 156

Charles the Great (Charlemagne), 95

Christianity, relation to Stoicism, 63, 75 f., 89; religion of Roman Empire, 69, 99; victory over competitors, 73; rise, 73, 75, 77; contribution to philosophy, 73, 80 ff., 103 f., 123; relation to Judaism, 73 f., 77, 80, 100; relation to Epicureanism, 75; relation to Plato, 73, 77 f., 86; ethics, 76; conversion of Justin, 77; relation to Neoplatonism, 78 f., 82, 86; relation to monasticism, 92; Porphyry as opponent, 94; relation to Aristotle, 98 f.; relation to Nominalism, 104; Renaissance, view of, 109; relation to Schopenhauer, 186

Clarke, Samuel, 161, 163

Cleanthes, 72

Coleridge, Samuel Taylor, 191

Columbus, Christopher, 109

Printed in Great Britain by The Riverside Press, Edinburgh

3.51